CW01523071

THE MECHANICS OF HUMAN PREJUDICE

This photograph, taken by a German photographer is called 'The Arrival' and shows three children and an old woman arriving in Auschwitz. The mother of the children will have been selected for slave labour while the old woman and the children are shown walking directly to the gas chambers. The same syndrome was displayed by Rwandans who hacked their neighbours to death in the marshes where they were hiding. This is a human characteristic displayed by human beings all over the world, not least by a US policeman who knelt on the back of a blameless fellow citizen until he suffocated. The aim of this work is not to allocate blame but is an attempt to understand the syndrome which causes this behaviour. It is not an easy or a simple read.

THE MECHANICS OF HUMAN PREJUDICE

The Paths to Social Sadism

Roger Nelson

About the Author
The author was born in 1933 near Leeds, Yorkshire. He went to school in England and Switzerland and did his National Service in REME in Germany before going to Downing College, Cambridge where he got a degree in Engineering. Since this is a book about prejudice it is only fair to say that he was brought up a Jew then married a Catholic and both are white. They have been married for over 50 years and have two sons. The family have travelled a good deal and have lived in the Far East, Middle East and Latin America. During one of the many slumps to hit the construction industry, he obtained a legal qualification and prepared, with others, commercial cases for litigation.

The Millrind Press 2022

3

THE MECHANICS OF HUMAN PREJUDICE
The Paths to Social Sadism
Copyright © Roger Nelson 2022

Published byThe Millrind Press

ISBN 978-1-902194-17-2

Disclaimer

Every effort has been made to ensure that the facts stated are as accurate as possible and supported by published works on the issue. Some of the works might be dated and intended only to educate and entertain. The author shall have no liability or responsibility to any person or entity regarding any loss or damage incurred, or alleged to have incurred, directly or indirectly, by information contained in this book.

Contents

Preface

If you can manage to read this far then you are a member of an English speaking human species called homo sapiens. There are no subdivisions. The behaviour of any human being can never be forecast with certainty, there are only tendencies and this work is about tendencies.

Because it is so much in the news at the moment and, since the 18th Century, it is worth recording right from the beginning that *race* does not exist. What does exist is humans of different appearance from the host body of the region they happen to be living in.[1] This struck a taxonomist called Carl Linnaeus (1707-1778) as a matter of significance and he mentioned it in passing. Nobody at that time expected race to be elevated to the position of a pseudoscience which it occupies at the present time (2022). Human appearance does not convey any human quality such as intelligence or, indeed, lack of intelligence; or the ability to earn a living in the environment in which we happen to be living but the more intelligent of us can learn. Some of us live longer than others. This has nothing to do with either superiority or inferiority

---

[1] An American actress made this point in 2022 and was derided for it.

but it has a lot to do with the environment, social distance and access to good medicine and a health service together with an absence of stress.

Those who cause stress by put downs at one end of the spectrum, going through reminders that the victim does not 'belong', on to personal insults is shortening the victim's life by an indefinable amount without it being a criminal offence. When the offender goes on to bodily harm or murder, then that does qualify as a criminal as a criminal offence. All these degrees of causing stress are on a spectrum referred to here as 'social sadism'.

The oldest depictions of the world human beings lived in are to be found in cave paintings which are fairly recent being no more than approximately 15, 000 years old. At Altamira, in Spain, huge bison and woolly mammoths are shown surrounded by signs which have been interpreted as male and female fertility symbols. No bones of these creatures are to be found at or near the cave and so it must be assumed that these are magic totems of great power used to guide the hunters to herds of smaller animals, like antelope, which could be hunted. Totem worship lasted into Christianity where the god Dagon, big fish, was used to guide fishermen to the shoals of fish in the Mediterranean sea. The parable of Jonah being swallowed by a big fish was reduced to writing as late as 700BCE and is an example, for the benefit of the people of Israel, of the power of the Almighty over the totem gods which still, at that time, covered the countryside. There were fertility gods like the golden calf and the serpent; the

8

god of war, (beit lehem); the god of leprosy (beit she'an) among, probably many others. No thorough study has yet been done but gods of this kind turn up all over the world. It is a phase that homo sapiens goes through and we are all the same.

Much closer to the matter in hand; prejudice against people of a different appearance has, at its root, the desire which everyone has, to feel they are worthy members of society. That they earn a living; that they have children in holy wedlock; that they comply with the local customs in every regard. It is common knowledge that many prefer to live and love others of the same gender. Unfortunately, some popular religions, without explanation, condemn any same sex love as a sin though, in truth, it is simply a physiological matter and as normal as having, say, blue eyes. Wealth is considered, in itself, a virtue possibly because a wealthy male used to be able to command a number of fertile females and his wealth gave him power. This is certainly the case with chimpanzees and so it might just be the case with humans. Certainly the virtuous maid gets the prince. She need not necessarily be a great beauty but some sort of virtue is essential. She stands by her man. Again, unfortunately taxonomy is part of a human instinct to categorise and create hierarchies. They place people who look like them at the top and those who look least like them at the bottom of a human hierarchy. In a white skinned society, this places black skinned humans at the bottom together with Jews who for special reasons are always placed at the bottom in Christian societies. In Britain, there is no overt cruelty in this and they are shown great

9

condescension as Lady Catherine de Bourgh[2] might have said. On this argument the preference people have for someone like themselves is based on tribal loyalty and if we marry someone who looks like ourselves, he or she might be a distant cousin and grant greater fertility.

These biases are institutionalised and those of a different appearance are rounded on at times of hardship when the main population feel out of control. Many, but not all, of those with less insight take to abusing those who do not look like the majority population because, when abusing and insulting they are in control. Jews, who frequently look quite similar to the majority population, have been subjected to Christian propaganda which, like any propaganda, removes normal empathy and allows a duty to kill to emerge.

The corollary of this is simply that anyone who does not look like 'us' is undesirable and could be an enemy. This is primitive reasoning seated in our limbic system but it takes a more sinister turn when an individual also feels humiliated. This is not true of everyone but those with low self esteem and who have internalised, ie believe in, their own lack of social status, are particularly vulnerable and project their humiliation on to somebody lower down the hierarchy than themselves (in their minds). The most numerous of these humiliated people are the poor and during extended periods of recession or austerity the poor project their anger at, typically, people of a different appearance, women, Jews and foreigners generally who do not speak like them. The

---

[2] Character in Pride and prejudice by Jane Austen.

economy makes them bullies. Politicians make use of this syndrome by saying that they too want to remove some of those at the bottom of the hierarchy. The cry of 'I am going to make Germany great again' rang through Europe in 1933 and proved irresistible to many of the poor of Germany but not all. What follows is a more detailed argument of what has been said above.

Section 1: The operation of the human brain

This may come as a surprise to the reader, as it did to the author, that every human being has three brains. An ancient stem brain which allows us to live and runs the heart, lungs and allows us to sleep. A limbic system of several parts which reacts very quickly to any situation with fear, anger and desire: i.e. the emotions. A third area which is not used as often as it ought to be does our long term reasoning. The cleverest people are those who can bypass the emotions and do the cold blooded reasoning. If they have power and whether they do that reasoning for good or evil is always a matter for debate. The great contribution to bypassing the emotions and hence logical reasoning came from the Greeks and the invention of mathematics in the 3rd and 4th Centuries BCE. In the 9th Century, great Islamic thinkers invented algebra. Philosophy was an attempt to reason in words and principles of social behaviour which came to its peak with the Greeks and, at the beginning of the First Century with the work of the Nazarenes in Galilee. There is little else except the emergence of the contemplative religions in about 500 BCE and, in England not until George Fox in the 17th Century. The popular religions have remained

12

welded to an all powerful, invisible god who will look after you providing you follow his ritual. It prompted Karl Marx to say:' *Religion is the opium of the people. It is the sigh of the oppressed creature, the heart of a heartless world, and the soul of our soulless condition.*' The gin riots and fear of the mob which gave way to universal emancipation possibly had more effect on common humanity than philosophy.

It goes almost without saying that all people who have ever been born were born as a result of the sexual instinct without which the human race would not exist. Humans are animals below the waist but can be brilliant above the waist. This dichotomy was not lost on the ancient Greeks who, it is thought took their first contact with mounted nomads to be centaurs. It cannot be over emphasised that every person alive today, and every person able to read this page, was born of a woman and are members of the same species. This has been so for hundreds of thousands of years. After many hominids had appeared and disappeared, homo sapiens appeared some 200,000 years ago, was consigned by anthropologists to a subgroup in the order of primates which itself dates from more than 63 mya, in the family hominidae. We humans share this sub group with the chimpanzee and the bonobo.

Eight million years ago open grassland appeared and the mammals existing at that time, including the horse, adapted to grassland whilst, in the jungles of what we now call Africa, six million years ago, lived various ape species. As recently as one hundred thousand years ago there were as many as six pre-humans species existing, known to anthropologists. There might have been more, living side by side, until the present day when only homo sapiens survived. The strength of sapiens is his survival instinct lodged in the limbic part of the human brain. This part of the brain reacts very rapidly to danger. The higher cortex reacts more slowly to mature thought.

While the stem brain keeps all mammals alive it is the limbic brain which reacts to danger or perceived danger and makes instant decisions without any reference to the higher part of the brain called the cerebral cortex The Cortex permits the power of reason but, for many, is little called upon. They have made up their minds, as they say. The limbic brain detects danger and calls on the 'fight or flight' reaction without reference to the cortex and without reasoned argument. For most people, their reasoning is emotional and quickly leads to anger as if their very survival is perceived as threatened. For any politician wishing to be elected in a democracy, they have to be elected by appealing to, or at least understanding, the emotions. It is not a system which should be denigrated and a number of very effective politicians have been elected in this way in the last one hundred years. It must also be said that the democratic system has, built within it, a weakness. The average British voter cannot resist voting for a politician who agrees with him. This is known as populism and is a stance beloved of many voters who believe in human appearance having some fundamental virtue or impurity rather than as fellow human beings with ability and value. Politicians have such faith in the importance of appearance that they turn themselves into caricatures, one, recently, wearing cloth cap and drinking pints of stout. A sensible electorate dismissed this performance as 'patronising' and removed their vote. Fortunately, the democratic system subjects every decision by the executive to debate and a vote in the House, both upper and lower chambers, before it becomes law.

The average English speaker can only hope that the politician who leads the party does not fully believe in the emotional appeal he is trying to make. However, it must be reiterated that when the leader and the electorate are some way down the path to narcissism, then bloody chaos can ensue as it did in Germany in the 1930s. This is the well recognised weakness of the democratic system and the separation of powers is essential to control excess power falling into the wrong hands as it has done in Russia in several Centuries. In the UK, only certain vestiges of the Royal Prerogative remain with the Crown so that only the Supreme Court can oppose the Executive as it did in 2019 to prevent the prorogation of parliament. For safety, it would make sense that a third domain of power should be added to the British constitution, whether written or agreed by custom.

With apologies for repeating this, because it is so important and frequently beyond our control, the limbic brain reacts rapidly with strong emotions like anger or tears because it is there to assist survival. Within the limbic system there is also seated that part of the brain called the amygdala. It is the part of the limbic system which has received the most study because it processes memory, decision making and emotional responses to events including fear, anxiety and anger and, most importantly, reward. The amygdala has a part to play in processing events as they happen to every individual without exception.

The use of the latest and most sophisticated part of the brain which sits on top of the limbic brain and is called the cerebral cortex is the only part of the brain which requires conscious effort to use. This effort is sometimes called 'thinking things through'. The strength of the contemplative religions is that they dull the activity of the amygdala and allow time for the cortex to work.

The operation of the limbic brain, gives rise to the appearance of an emotion.[3] The appearance of an emotion is accompanied by a facsimile thought process one aspect of which has been discerned as Simmel's rule.

> 'The stranger is close to us , insofar as we feel between
> him and ourselves common features of a national social,
> occupational, or generally human, nature. He is far from
> us, insofar as these common features extend beyond him
> or us, and connect us only because they connect a great
> many people.

> — Georg Simmel, "The Stranger" (1908)

It is by relying on Simmel that the populist politician finds an easy route to power. He poses as the stranger who has common sympathies of a national nature. One of the great

---

[3] Taken from Marc Scheon "Your Survival Instinct is Killing You" and Thomas lewis et al. "A General Theory of Love."

populists of the 20th Century, Adolf Hitler, posed as someone who saw 'the Jew' and 'communism' as a common threat to national existence. His speeches along these lines carried him to power together with his appearance as the common man, an old soldier who had fought for his country. None of this had any bearing on whether he was suitable to occupy a position of power which, in the event, he was not.

Having chosen a hero or a villain it is with great reluctance that such a person is abandoned in spite of all the evidence against him or her. One of the ways such a person is installed as a hero or villain is by means of the conspiracy theory. The conspiracy is headed by an alien power of considerable strength and, surprisingly the BBC have been cast in this role. The ex leader of the Labour Party was accused of allowing a left wing group within his party to make anti Semitic remarks. Eleven members of the Labour Party resigned the party whip over anti Jewish remarks made by groups within the Labour Party. Labour lost badly in the 2019 general election and faithful party members put this down to a Jewish conspiracy within the BBC blowing a few trivial remarks out of proportion and naming two or three Jewish newscasters.[4] This syndrome is called denial and is indulged in by those with a narcissistic personality of individuals within the Labour Party caused by, possibly in their case, the shame of poverty. There are a multitude of causes of shame and they vary with time and the society a human happens to find him or herself in. What follows shame is

---

[4] For an exposé of this syndrome, Judith Ornstein; Whitewashed Anti-Semitism in the Labout Party.

what is called in this book: social sadism. It involves shouting or sneering at a weaker individual of a different appearance, physical violence against a weaker individual such as a woman; finally, murder committed against a weaker individual. Even warfare against a weaker nation falls under this category such as Germany against certain European nations and, very recently, Russia's attack on Ukraine both fall under this category.

The conspiracy always involves an alien power of massive strength (the BBC controlled by Jews) which only the hero can overcome. Beowulf, for example, is such a hero, from an Old English epic poem composed in the 7th Century in East Anglia. Wise and incredibly brave Beowulf is protecting the peaceful countryside of Heorot from Grendel, a ferocious giant with burning eyes and a body covered in armoured scales. Grendel snatches men from their beds and tears them limb from limb. As though this were not enough, Grendel has an even more monstrous mother. Only Beowulf, a Saxon, can conquer them using a sword forged by giants.[5] This is, of course, pure fiction but it is used, or something like it, to justify the way 'we' stood alone against a monstrous foe whoever 'we' may be. The lack of factual evidence is ignored but the Hero is the politician proposing to rescue the nation from a foreigner threatening it. "Patriotism is the last refuge of a scoundrel" as Dr Johnson memorably said. It has to be said that Grendels do appear from time to time and they portray their victims as monsters like themselves and cannot see that this is denial gone berserk. As many who have used

---

[5] Taken from Rob Brotherton Suspicious Minds

18

their cerebral cortex have experienced, mature reflection moderates the initial reaction and the emotions frequently moderate with time as the world came to realise after Germany's love affair with Adolf Hitler in 1939.

The problem human beings have is that the emotional reaction they feel was learned in a world which has long since disappeared and with a global population which existed before the population explosion of approximately one thousand years ago; but it still rules us from its grave [6], as F W Maitland might have said. Our fast primitive reaction still recognises anyone who does not look like the observer as an enemy. Someone who looks like the observer is taken as a friend. This was illustrated to some extent by the truce brought about during Christmas 1914 by enlisted men, particularly the British and the Germans who came cautiously out of their trenches and spent two or three days, burying their dead, exchanging gifts and jokes while their generals plotted the continuation of the war and closing any truce down.[7] The event was poorly reported in the London press as though it was a cowardly act rather than a possible opportunity for peace. The need to recognise a friend or a foe before befriending or killing them is illustrated from the fact that the British army has never won a war against guerilla fighters. The second Boer war, 1899-1902, shook Britain to a considerable extent when a British army was defeated by the descendants of Dutch settlers. This event alone made discerning politicians like Sir Edward Grey suspect that the

---

[6] F.W.Maitland 1850-1906
[7] Stanley Weintraub, Silent Night.

19

Empire was beginning to crumble and he saw the answer in alliances as did the Germans, both of whom saw alliances as a way of preserving the balance of power in Europe. He formed the triple entente of France, Russia and Britain, in the event, against the triple alliance of Germany, Austria-Hungary and Italy. Russia and Italy soon dropped out and the ensuing blood bath made it clear that war is in nobody's interest.

Turning now to the more normal social events which begin violent relations between human beings

It seems that some life event triggers the operation of the limbic system when there is an actual threat but it directs it's fear and anger in the wrong direction and this seems to be the part cause of, at least, some of the common neurotic responses like anger, love, wife beating and stalking. More importantly the active limbic system releases a neurotransmitter called dopamine and natural opiates called endorphins which enable, as part of the survival mechanism, any human to continue operating when they should be in pain but only for a limited time. This seems to be the case whether the pain is physical or emotional. It is ironic that the very system that causes humans to feel fear causes humans, via the hypothalamus, to trigger off a chain reaction of biological changes among which are the production of more adrenalin for the purpose of fleeing or fighting. A curious reaction to stress of any kind is also a reduction of dopamine which allows pain to surface together with a drop in activity of the frontal lobes and it is this which can cause discomfort or even pain itself. The most frequent source of stress in a modern society is commanding fewer economic resources than your peer group or, as a group from London School of Economics led by Lorenza Antonucci perceptively said, in relation to Brexit, *a threat to their lifestyle*. This applies to rich and poor alike and the pain is alleviated by bullying someone weaker than the person under stress. 'Weaker' in this sense means someone who has previously been exposed to hatred, ridicule or contempt and is accepted by many of the population as, in reality, being weaker. This is frequently no more than a myth but is believed in like holy writ by some members of the population who need to feel better about themselves.

Mammals have developed a mental state called limbic resonance whereby one person becomes attuned to another's mental state.[8] In this way prejudice and opinions are passed from generation to generation with nothing being written down or even said. The political party which lifts a section of society, whether coal miners or mill workers, out of poverty will have their loyalty at the ballot box for generations to come. In the 1980s the main source of power in Britain was coal. At the same time, inflation was high and was being combatted by raising interest rates. This produced a drop in GDP, in other words, a recession. Mining, which was a nationalised industry, had such power that even the threat of a strike could produce a pay offer and their loyalty to their Union the NUM, produced by years of hardship when only it stood between them and starvation in the 1930s,

---

[8] A General Theory of Love, Lewis et al. p.63

50 years earlier, was such that when they struck it was rock solid and only a tiny minority continued working. The incoming Conservative government finally solved the impasse by closing the collieries and importing coal from Poland. The miner's loyalty to their union, even though the economic situation had changed from the 1930s, was down to limbic resonance. They had learned over generations that the Union and sticking together was the solution to the inhumanity of the coal owners.

It may be some sort of resonance which produces a response when a human looks into the face of another mammal, even a dog or a cat, while there is no response at all when looking into the eye of a reptile or a fish because, it is believed, these creatures have no limbic system.[9] Among humans, eye contact can be perceived over several yards and evokes an emotional response not always favourable. The effect of eye contact is enhanced partly because the human eye is surrounded by white which indicates clearly which way the eye is looking. Under normal circumstances the effect of eye contact is favourable. A British ambassador, whose private opinion of the American President was that he was inept, dysfunctional with a divided administration also noticed that when Trump, the president in question, entered a room, he made eye contact with everyone and made them all feel special.

'He has star quality' he said.[10] This quality is not laudable in itself but it reinforces the respect which humans have

---

[9] A General Theory of Love, Lewis et al. p.42
[10] Kim Darroch in an interview with Newsnight 8 Sept 2020

inherited from their tribal past for a leader. It is similar to the respect for him which a politician tries to establish with his electorate. It is for this reason that adultery in the life of any individual, particularly a politician, has to be concealed even though it might well have no relevance to his competence at the job in hand. In June 2021 a cabinet minister had to resign when photographed kissing a lady aide in front of an open window. There was no question of him being incompetent, merely the need to sell newspapers and public opinion. The same would have befallen H H Asquith 1852-1928, had his relationship with Venetia Stanley become public knowledge. In fact, it was the death toll on the Somme which caused him to resign of his own volition. Such morality can only be condemned on the grounds that, in a public servant, he does not have have his full attention on the task ahead of him. It has to be said that in any other walk of life, only professional incompetence would earn him dismissal.

Many people invent a stereotype for themselves which includes, for example; being the member of a particular political party; more prudent at handling the economy; led by the rich; churchgoers. The sort of stereotype most Victorian novelists would have recognised. On the other hand they can be champions of the poor; believers in equality; opposed to privilege;   closing schools which rely on selection by examination; led by and represented by Unions led by men. These stereotypes are always out of date, sometimes by several hundreds of years. For example, many people, who have persuaded themselves that they are socially inferior because their forebears were farm workers, will vote with a right wing political party so as to promote the illusion that they are patriots. Logically, the voter most feared in politics is the 'floating' voter who votes either in his own best interests or in the nation's best interests or, he might, on many occasions, vote for both. With great perspicacity, the Conservative Party persuaded a number of Labour held constituencies in the Midlands, Yorkshire, North East Wales and Northern England to switch to them by promising more investment being channelled in their direction. This was particularly persuasive in 2017 because of the years of Conservative policy of trying to balance the books thereby restricting the money supply and causing the austerity people were tired of. Again, it is ironic that the party whose Chancellors had played an important role in perpetuating austerity, was the one to benefit from the discontent which their handling of the economy had created in the first place.

The answer to these political reactions is always to activate the cerebral cortex with reasoned arguments which, it has been shown, will frequently reduce anxiety and the activity of the limbic system once the cause of the anxiety has been understood. Another way to do this, it has been observed, is via meditation.[11] or other thoughtful process rather than preaching which the thoughtful have always treated with caution. Meditation lowers the activity of the amygdala and allows the brain more time to think. This has always proved to be more difficult for human beings than it sounds possibly because we admire those with power and because the rational reasoning system in the cortex is walled off in some way from

---

[11] Ibid page 72

the limbic system with the emotions and requires persuasion to consider any question. A huge hole has been blown into this ancient belief that tribal leaders deserve respect by the recent pandemic when the opinions of experts carried more weight than the elected politicians and the media who provided platforms for the experts gained in power.

Section 2: The development of the human survival Instinct.

The human survival instinct, led by the emotions, has been developed over the last hundreds of thousands of years and allows hominid and, finally, humans to jump to instant conclusions based on life in an environment which disappeared many years ago. The species ability to recognise danger is based entirely on appearance. Within living memory the tribes of Africa could be recognised by their hair styles and facial tattoos. Clothing marked the different ranks of the individuals within the tribe. British costume from Roman times denoted the rank of the individual by the weapons he carried particularly the shield. Druids wore distinctive ornaments in a horse shoe shape. All this so that our rank could be recognised within the tribe and due deference paid. Appearance was and is, everything. After appearance, for many of us, a stereotype kicks in and we still have no idea who we are dealing with.

The society we all came from has gone through a small number of phases since its inception some two hundred thousand years ago: living like apes in what is now Africa about which relatively little is known at the moment; living as hunter gatherers and nomads, all over the world about which a great deal is known or inferred from surviving small hunter-gatherer societies who are being deprived of their territories at the present time and finally the technically advanced societies themselves in which we live at the present time controlled by money supply and prices.

With considerable perspicacity, primitive human beings recognised that survival depended on fertility and food. The standing stones which represented our ancestors were a particular form of celebrating the land which sustained us and to which they were fixed and a celebration of the length of time we had lived there as a family and as a nation. Immigrants do not belong 'here', wherever 'here' might be. Standing stones appeared in England, France, Scotland, Ireland and Northern Europe. They seem to have occurred where food came from the land because the ancestors were fixed to the land and they had also defended the land against foreign tribes who had tried to invade. Megaliths are found to a possible lesser extent, in many places over the world but none to the same extent as Egypt where huge structures are fixed to the land. A possibly earlier phase began for humans some 20,000 years ago with drawings on the walls of caves, not necessarily inhabited caves, showing carefully observed animals, mainly horses and bison, some might have been depicted as having human heads.[12] In zones where there were no rocks, there was a huge effort made to haul in large stones, sometimes from many miles away. Failing the availability of rock, even at a distance, or within a society without the

---

12 Genevieve von Petzinger The First Signs

surplus resources to haul rock, wooden posts were resorted to, decorated and became totems. By far the most frequently encountered form of totem was cave drawings. Totems were essential to life and were among other things, dedicated to food or fertility or both. The cave drawings might then be totems which guided early man to the herds for hunting purposes. It is most unlikely that tribes could afford to share their food with men or women maintained for purely artistic, purposes, like subsistence a priesthood, who did the drawings. In addition to the drawings, there were found numerous figurines of voluptuous women used, very probably, as fertility totems. The shape alone indicating they were producing oestrogen just as it does today in the case of female celebrities. The mere shape of men and women provides an industry, the fashion industry, for hundreds of thousands of people who worship celebrities for the reason among many others, than that they have what seems to be the ideal amount of subcutaneous fat with a slender waist. It is true that many celebrities have massive ability as singers or dancers but many see their careers falter, even end, when their waists thicken. It is a universal language which transcends nationality.

'To be reproductively successful, ancestral men had to marry women with the capacity to bear children'[13]

The way in which a woman of any appearance or background displays her reproductive capacity is to have an hour glass figure which shows she is producing oestrogens.

---

[13] Workman and Reader, Evolutionary Psychology p.94

Oestrogens develop breasts, hips and thighs and put fat on buttocks. When a woman reaches menopause there is a tendency for the fat to migrate to the waist and abdomen. In spite of being hundreds of thousands of years old and in many ways no longer relevant, this desire still rules a great part of human behaviour and, as a result, there is now a global multi billion dollar fashion industry. The Venus of Lespugue found in 1922 in the Grotte des Rideaux dating from the Upper Paleolithic is a statuette showing a woman with massive buttocks and, possibly, pregnant.[14] Large buttocks in some women today are more the product of male choice over several generations than physiology.

If the human species has inherited this primitive instinct, an obsession with sexuality, from its animal forebears, all well and good because without it or something like it, the specie would not exist. There is no reason why humans should not share the chimpanzee's territoriality to increase the supply of fertile females through food. The need to survive is built in to any living organism because, without it, they would not be here. When the environment changes, some species die out and global warming is killing species at a frightening rate.

The possession of a fertile woman is a sign of controlling territory and territory is important because it is a sign of power. It indicates to the primitive mind a high status male who can command both territory and females. American politicians tend to impress the electorate with these symbols more than the British and it has the advantage that no

---

[14] Ivar Lissner Illustrations 70/71 Man, God and Magic.

reasoned speeches need be involved. It is no more than following a strong animal leader to ensure survival. The practice of successful men acquiring a younger woman, either as a wife or a mistress is so prevalent that such a woman has been dubbed 'the trophy wife'. She is usually acquired on retirement and her acquisition is designed to reassure the male that he is still a force to be reckoned with.

Earlier figurines were inscribed with a triangle to indicate the delta of Venus and 'three' persisted as a magic number because tens of thousands of years ago the triangle was a symbol of fertility. Birth is so important, a birth goddess appeared in what might have been a special birth cavern. Food and children are essential to human survival and both myth and magic are devoted to these two ends. The role of the male in Neanderthal society, 200,000 years ago, seems to have been no more than the provision of sperm and a Neanderthal female in estrus copulated with multiple males so that the stongest sperm inseminated the ovary. This, apparently led to genetic variation including changes in the skin.[15] A genetic mutation MCIR, for example, produces light skinned children.[16]

One of the most powerful totems ever described is to be found in the Old Testament in the book of Judges, the story of Samson who destroyed the Temple of Dagon which dates from some 5,000 years ago. 'Dag' is the Semitic word for fish and 'Dagon' simply means 'Big Fish'. The parable of

---

[15]   Svante Paabo, Neanderthal man p.213.
[16]   Nina Jablonski, Skin. footnote Chapter 6

Jonah in the Old Testament takes on a clearer meaning, namely, that even from the depths of a foreign totem, a true believer will still hear the word of God. The priests of Dagon had the bodies of a fish with the head of a man crowned with with the head of a fish which has survived today in the shape of a bishop's mitre. This creature was the totem which guided the Philistines and probably others around the Mediterranean to the fish shoals in the sea. Other totems can be seen referred to in the Old Testament apart from Dagon. Beit Lehem, which became Bethlehem in English translations is probably the home of the god of war; Beit She'an is probably the home of a totem which protects one from leprosy, a greatly feared disease. The name Naḥson, anglicised to Nelson, indicates a follower of the snake totem, the serpent being a phallic symbol. The name Samson indicated a follower of the sun totem. The famous Samson from the bible had also taken the Nazirite vow not to take alcoholic drink and not to cut his hair. The totems indicate the important factors in ancient life, notably fertility. With better food and more copious food, fertility is, in reality, less important though the sex instinct is built into us and some can even become deranged if deprived of it.

Christianity became a world religion and in the course of this happening it absorbed the totemic faiths of Europe. At one time, the symbol for Christian was a fish. When Christianity arrived in Rome it took over a bull cult whose priests were eunuchs and the bull (impersonated by a human male) was reincarnated after three days. The early Christians, not to be outdone, also introduced a human god who was reincarnated after three days.

The other important decision maker in the human limbic brain is the population explosion which took place one thousand[17] years ago.[18] Relatively suddenly the supply of food increased and, with a better diet, women became more fertile. In England and Wales, between 1000 and 1500 AC the population trebled and Thomas Malthus (1766-1834) despaired of Britain, as it was by then, ever reaching the stage of universal prosperity. As agriculture became more mechanised and efficient, it was consumed by increases in the population. Every holiday was accompanied by a surge in births. Apart from sex, the need for children, particularly boys who could work the land was a way of providing for old age. For this reason boys have been preferred to girls because they could work the land, even though not their own land, and provide for their parents in their old age.

Very recently, as late as 1960, women took birth control into their own hands, the state took over care in old age and the Health Service made it their sacred duty to extend life as long as possible. Such social factors ensured a lower birth rate and the fertility rate has gone from 5.5 births per woman in 1820 to 1.75 births per woman in 2020. True, many more children survive to adulthood today than they did in 1820, and the number of live births needed to maintain the population is 2.1 births per woman. In spite of any information to the contrary, the limbic brain continues to function in the overcrowded squalor of Victorian England when anyone who did not look look like us or talk like us

---

17 Allen W Johnson et al The Evolution of Human Societies ... Location 178
18 A General Theory of Love p.63

could be an enemy. Those who do look like 'us' and talk like 'us' are taken to belong to the land like standing stones and are entitled to be here but anyone else might be masquerading for their own purposes. This suspicion persists into the present time when, in reality, we are in need of immigrants to provide the slack in the economy needed to avoid inflation and, as a suspicion or, indeed, a certainty, is adopted by those of lower intellect who feel out of control. It was this certainty which took the UK out of Europe. The clever slogan used at the time was 'Take Back Control'. No rational argument was required.

Though described here as primitive, it is not far removed from recent times in this country. When Ruth Williams married Seretse Kharma, paramount chief of the Bamengwato Tribe of Bechuanaland in 1948, they had difficulty finding an Anglican clergyman to perform the ceremony and Daniel Malan, Prime Minister of South Africa described the marriage as 'nauseating'. Marrying a black skinned man in spite of his education and intelligence was seen as a betrayal of her tribe and nation in the eyes of many white people. There may, however be a somewhat more statistical basis, though equally illogical reason for choosing, as a mate, someone who looks like you and talks like you, based on increased female fertility that is, having more children. Many societies in the Middle East, where population densities are low and have been low for thousands of years have encouraged consanguineous marriage on the grounds that a girl is happier and more secure surrounded by her family. This could well be a social norm dating from thousands of years ago to increase the population. An Icelandic study[19] found that the size of families decline as genetic remoteness increased. Between 1800 and 1824 3rd Cousins had 4.04 children per couple and 9.17 grandchildren. 8th Cousins on the other hand had 3.34 children per couple and 7.31 grandchildren. The chances of a recessive gene carrying on to the next generation has been calculated as 1 in 16 for siblings down to 1 in 64 for first cousins. This might indicate that, as has been seen to be the case, in small communities, a 1 in 16 chance of ill health would be noticed after a few generations, which would explain why small communities encouraged the sort of prostitution mentioned above.

Wise women have developed from choosing a mere sexual partner to looking for a good provider who will see them through the months of pregnancy, though this latter need is waning in the modern world as the advent of a highly technical society makes brains and education as important as muscle power.

The phase in our history as members of the human species has a long period as hunter gatherers which still exerts an emotional pull as, in some respects, an ideal though, in reality, not many would want to go back to it. One of the most striking aspects of hunter gatherer life in its nomadic form is the lack of reliance on material wealth and the alleged equality between the genders

---

[19] Reported by Audrey Grayson, ABC News Medical Unit 2008

Robert L Kelly in his book The Lifeways of Hunter-Gatherers Location 543 summarises the characteristics of the hunter-gatherer society which can be further summarised as follows:

1. Egalitarianism. Mobility constrains the amount of property that can be owned and thus serves to maintain material equality.

2. Low population density. Population is kept below carrying capacity through intentional, conscious controls such as abstention, abortion, and infanticide

3. Lack of territoriality. Long-term adaptation to resource variability requires that Hunter-gatherers be able to move from one region to another, making defended territories maladaptive.

4. A minimum of food storage. Since the group is nomadic and food plentiful relative to population density (see characteristic 2), food storage is unnecessary; hence the potential of storage to create social hierarchy is thwarted.

5. Flux in band position. Maintaining social ties requires frequent movements and visiting, which also discourages violence since disputes can be solved through group fissioning rather than fighting.

It must therefore be the arrival of agronomy in any particular society which produced male supremacy. The desirability of well watered farmland means that it would have to be both worked and defended from invaders and this would place physical strength and courage at a premium. The

35

attractiveness of physical strength and courage is still with us even when it has been completely replaced by the ability to earn a living in the society in which people find themselves.

Section 3: Empathy

Empathy is a strong fellow feeling for people who look like us and talk like us whoever 'us' might be when 'us' are in danger or pain. When the people in danger or pain do not look like us then most right thinking people feel sympathy but nothing stronger than that. The mammal system of survival is to live in groups called, in the human case, families. The purpose of the family is to bring up the young until they can survive on their own. An interesting experiment is called 'the cliff' in which a baby, accompanied by it's mother crawls along a wooden counter which turns to glass. The baby looks at it's mother and if the mother looks smiling and confident, the baby will frequently crawl out on to the glass which is perfectly safe. This is the beginning of empathy. Reading the expression on the face of a family member to see whether there is danger. The arrangement is reciprocal and if the baby perceives danger or is in pain, a family member will come to it's aid. Many mothers cannot bear to allow prolonged crying from their baby. The reading of mother's expression and the reciprocal feeling she has for her baby might explain why women might have more empathy than men. If this is true, it means that all human beings have empathy. This would make it difficult if not impossible for humans to go to war, particularly if the people they are told to kill are those who look like them and talk like them. In theory, this would make civil war impossible but in actuality this is demonstrably not so. For governments, this difficulty is overcome by propaganda. In the American Civil War there was cartoon emphasis on the inhumanity of the South's treatment of blacks. Both sides called on patriotism and the South recruited in the name of the Colonel of the regiment, a decent, family man just like you!

The greater the disparity in language or appearance between the two sides, the easier it is to go to war. In the First World War, the only difference between the British and Germans was the language. Even so the Germans, on Christmas Eve 1914, sang carols and both sides came out to bury the dead, exchange presents, cigarettes and play football. In quiet parts of the line there persisted a live and let live policy in which any shooting was restrained.

As Ponsonby[20] and the Quakers persistently claimed: "*WWI had no basis in law and no political necessity*". It might well have arisen out of the humiliation of the Kaiser at Cowes and his withered arm coupled with the sincere belief that extending territory made the tribe more powerful and this could only be done by war. This latter no longer has any relevance and territory has been replaced by trade. It seems humans feel empathy for every other living creature and propaganda has to be used extensively to get humans to kill other humans now that territory has become irrelevant

---

[20] Arthur Ponsonby, Falsehood in Wartime.

38

propaganda has come to the fore as it did in times gone by. The more primitive the people being appealed to the more primitive the standing of the need for war. Mr Putin, appealed to the old Bolshevik generation when he said the invasion of Ukraine was necessary to protect them from being taken over by Nazis in order to provide a casus belli for a Russian invasion of Ukraine in 2022. At once this split Russia in two: the elderly who favoured war and the young who favoured peace and risked prison sentences when they protested. Nor did it diminish in any way, the importance of propaganda as old ladies, hiding in cellars in East Ukraine that the fighting was instigated by America because they needed the land for nuclear purposes.

The interest in Europe is because Ukraine is a European country and, it is alleged, Ukrainians have white skin and look like us. As a result, Ukraine is on the news every day for most of the day. In contrast, a proxy war has been waged in Yemen since 2012 when the acting President, Abbrabuh Mansur Hadi, was overthrown by Houthi militants supported by Iran and 100,000 have died is rarely ever reported on British news. Hadi is supported by Saudi Arabia and, from time to time, USA and UK. The Yemenis have dark skin but it must be accepted both wars are equally dangerous and must be stopped if possible.

Of more recent wars from Korea onward, the most tragic was the attack on Afghanistan by the US in 2001. Afghanistan is part, a major part, of the Pashtun empire which extends from within Iran, across Afghanistan, through the Kyber Pass to the Indus basin in Pakistan. The entire area has multiple governments but only one language: Pashto. US and European troops who were there to support the Afghan Northern Alliance speak not a word of Pashto and in a guerilla war against Pashto speaking fighters raised in Pakistan, they were at a grave disadvantage. A similar empire could be made up of the English speaking nations except that in the technically advanced economies, nationality has been replaced by trade and nations are now run for the benefit of huge, multinational conglomerates. Many of them unknown to the general public but the top 500 have a turnover of 33 trillion. This is ten times the turnover of the UK. The legality of what turned out to be a Nato intervention is also difficult to understand because Nato is a defensive organisation, not an invasion force.

In war, empathy is withdrawn by both sides and families are murdered. Both sides find this easier if the killing is remote; carried out by aerial bombardment or rockets. Much more distressing when the killer is face to face with his victim. The Germans started murdering Jewish peasants by machine gun after they had dug their own mass graves during the invasion of Poland in 1942. There is a story that a Jewish mother held up her child from the mass of dead bodies and a passing Polish woman rescued it from her arms. The Polish woman showed empathy and, it must be said, courage. No empathy existed for doomed children wearing their best clothes, standing on the ramp at Auschwitz and photographed by meticulous German photographers. The propaganda provided by the Christian church over a long period of time

40

was such as to make the annihilation of the Jews a public duty. By no means did every German believe this but those made to suffer great shame believed it absolutely. There is more on the combination of shame, narcissism and sadism later in this essay.

Section 4: Shame

Shame arises as a result of an individual's failure to equal or exceed a social norm. The most common norms in the UK are based on appearance, sexuality and personal wealth. They are so powerful that, in spite of being essentially trivial, were adopted by religion for either redundant or ignoble reasons and, in this way, assumed a moral dimension and those who could comply with the norms were considered and thought of themselves as better people. A young woman who had just met a local millionaire who had come to live in the village said: 'I cannot help myself, I treat rich people with more respect'. She had internalised her own inferiority vis a vis those who were richer than her. It follows then that those who fail to comply with certain norms, providing they had internalised the system, feel shame.

The most common norm in former times was having white skin. As little as 100 years ago the mere possession of white skin got one a better job; and white skinned people believed in it for the obvious reason that it was in their interests to do so. The British Empire was a trade edifice which brought wealth to many, but not all, and was maintained by British military power to obtain raw materials for British factories mainly in Lancashire. In days gone by, many people were looked down on for the colour of their skin, their religion, sexuality and wealth, or their command of credit. When those that cannot comply with any or all of those norms believed they actually were inferior, they were said to have internalised it. That is to say, they actually believed the propaganda the white population were putting out.

It might be difficult to believe but internalisation did and does exist. Those who feel shame, seek to ease the burden by projecting it on to some other group who are subjected to adverse propaganda, frequently, in Christian countries it is Jews upon whom shame is projected and whom Christianity portrays as the murderers of the Christian saviour. Incredible as it might now seem, as little as 100 years ago, women were considered intellectually inferior to men and a man who needed a wife who went out to work was considered, and considered himself, inferior. In countries with failed economies, the shame of poverty is projected on to women. A school girl , Malala Yousafzai, was shot in the face by a Taliban because if she, a mere girl, got an education then what was he? With no one to project his failure on to, he was diminished.

In Britain, the denigration of people with darker skin began with the Indian Mutiny of 1857 when numbers of troops in the East India Company army mutinied against their British officers and were portrayed in the British press as rapists and murderers and the only way dealing with them was to kill them. A cartoon in Punch labelled 'Justice' by Sir John Tenniel shows Britannia standing atop a heap of black, inert bodies and slaughtering them with her sword. At this distance of time, it is difficult to say whether this is irony or a serious social injunction. The fiction then arose that black people were uncivilised and savages, lusting after the bodies of white women. Even during the Mutiny itself, there were only three or four examples of rape.[21] White supremacy became based on a civilising mission for those people with black skin, not only in India, but the whole world and certainly there were examples such as suttee which Indian women could usefully do without but resisted by men as interference, with their ancient customs[22] but to provide service in the afterlife. It could possibly have stemmed from an ancient custom in which the wife of a great warrior threw herself on his funeral pyre rather than live without him. In the 20th Century the women of the two dictators: Hitler and Mussolini chose to die with them because they were the greatest men they had ever known.

Even in the present time, there exist examples of women gaining status from the status of their husbands or partners. Equally, they can be ashamed of their husbands or partners and, as a result, display social sadism to reduce others to their level. However, in the case of suttee, women were not prepared to bring their lives to an early, painful end. Indeed, so unpopular with women was this custom, there seem to be examples of women being being physically stopped from escaping and being held down in the flames. Not surprisingly, the British described their mission in India, not as a trade

---

[21] Wikipedia: The Indian Mutiny
[22] Denis Judd Empire

mission to buy cheap raw material for factories in Lancashire but as one to civilise the black savage. It sounds more elevated than the bare truth and from this came the well known phrase and belief that civilising those with black skin was part of the white man's burden. The idea of white superiority has had tragic consequences for white people all over world. Led by their achievements in physics and equality, leaders in Britain, in spite of their technical superiority, have become, to a greater or lesser extent embroiled in wars generated by the US and lost. The latest being Afghanistan which is resolving itself at the time of writing. The price of losing being a continuation of Aid and corruption money, as in the past. Even this, if true, it would be preferable to war. Any compromise is preferable to war providing war has not broken out. Once war has broken out, compromise is more difficult because the dead cannot be allowed to have died in vain.

Until recently there existed a norm which stated that, as stated above, women were intellectually inferior to men. This is demonstrably untrue as a generality, nevertheless it is only slowly losing it's grip in the Western world and the Orient, it is still held to firmly in the Middle East which, with the exception of Israel, is one of the most technically backward regions of the world. The first mention of a woman is Eve in Genesis, created by God as a 'fitting helper' for Adam. It seems clear that she is not intended to be in charge.[23] Eve is guided by her phallic totem, a serpent, to the forbidden tree of knowledge. This seems, to the modern reader, a very good

---

[23]   Genesis 2 in the Jewish Study Bible

thing indeed but to some, it is still blasphemy to suggest that life is anything more than a bovine acceptance of fate or God's will. What is fairly clear is that it is Eve's job to have the children, essential to the perpetuation of the human race. To both men and women, totems were essential to regulate and make sense of the world they lived in. Eve could have children providing she was adequately fed and, as has already been noted, displayed subcutaneous fat as women do to this day. As George Bernard Shaw, the playwright, noted: this gives women so much power, it is fortunate they are physically weaker than men. In Saudi Arabia, if women show so much as an ankle under their gowns they can be whipped with a cane by some sort of morality police. Women have always given birth to about 5% more males than females but the death in childbirth of males and warfare left a preponderance of young females without husbands. This was particularly so in Britain after WWI but as a result of improved medical practices and lower death rate in war, there is now a preponderance of males and women can pick and choose their mate. Sad little associations of celibate males have sprung up partly from the change in numbers but partly from the fact that, due to equality of education, professional women equal or exceed men. Following the Industrial Revolution and electrical assisted control mechanisms men's superior strength has less economic value so that women are now, in every way the equal of men. Indeed, reports by Mckinsey, the management consultants, indicate that corporations with women on the board of directors make bigger profits than those with men only.[24] In spite of all the

[24] mary ann Sieghart: The Authority Gap p.77

numbers and facts on the ground, women still internalise their own lesser status. Lin Bian of the University of Illinois found from a series of story tests that, at the age of five, both boys and girls thought their own gender was the cleverer but by the age of seven there was a tendency to assign cleverness to men.[25] The reason for this might be brought about by limbic resonance whereby children learn the opinion of their elders from minute changes in expression when certain subjects are mentioned. It could be in this way, that racial hierarchies are maintained. Men with low self esteem, for whatever reason, believe that women should be below men and remain in their control and know their place. Such men will even kill if their self esteem is sufficiently diminished and in 2019, 1.6 million women suffered domestic abuse and, in Britain, two women per week are still murdered by their male partners. This is an extreme example of social sadism.

Poverty is a major source of shame because, historically, the poor lived in insanitary conditions and were closer to death than the middle class, who make up 75% of the population. The present difference in life expectancy between reasonably well off and not quite managing is about ten years. The difference in life expectancy between rich and poor has always been known to be based on lower stress, moderate diet (moderate sugar intake) and clean air. Anyone sitting on a bus or a tram in the 1930s and descending to centre of town would pass through a pall of black smoke. The mills at the bottom of the valley poured their effluent into the river so that it looked like a glittering black snake moving slowly to

---

[25] Ditto p.86 2017

the sea. The aim in life was to find a home above the layer of smoke and anyone below the smoke was a failure. It was this which defined the poor. In the 19th Century to this noxious mix could be added cholera. So obviously damaging to health was this state of affairs that the Yorkshire philanthropist Sir Titus Salt (1803-1876) moved his entire workforce from the slums of Bradford to a village he built for them well upstream to a place which he called Saltaire. It is said he watched from a tower to make sure they went to work and to church but he removed them from cholera. Every fairy story, including those published by Mills and Boon depicts a relatively impoverished girl who marries a prince attracted to her by her physical beauty rather than the fact that she has an honours degree in natural sciences from Cambridge University. This fairy tale is waning as women become more and more achievers in their own right without reliance on anyone. Nevertheless, among older women, the fairy tale persists and they are ashamed of husbands in low status jobs in social categories D and E: Semi skilled and unskilled manual workers; Casual or lowest grade workers, pensioners, and others who depend on the welfare state for their income. These two categories combined amount to nearly 25% of the population.

They are categories that unskilled immigrants occupy until they improve their status, those who can improve their status pass the native population who are left inventing conspiracy theories to explain their failure in the great race for status. It was, in part, the dwindling status of the native population that gave rise to Brexit. Foreigners were making money out of us and that was why our standard of living was declining.

Women with low status husbands show shame and resort to some degree of bullying manners and put downs to those they perceive as weaker than themselves. It is bullying or, more accurately, social sadism that brings relief to those who feel shame. The genteel Hyacinth Bucket comes to mind when faced by her family.

There exists a norm in Christian societies which says that a Christian marriage is a heterosexual marriage. Much the same exists in Judaism. In the Old Testament and taken up by many Christians, particularly Catholics to the present time, homosexuality was a sin which would deny a homosexual entry to the kingdom of heaven in the hereafter. This harsh, inhuman view was recorded as one of the abominations of Leviticus but was based on nothing more than rabbinical self interest at the time. Going back 3,000 years, shortly before the bible was reduced to writing, the US Census Bureau estimated World population at 50 million human beings. The present world population is estimated at 7,800 million so that whatever prompted religion to condemn same sex relationships as sinful, any logic has been abandoned and we are left with what looks like nothing more than self-interest by the clergy. Population was everything, homosexuality among Jews is nominally forbidden and, in rabbinic law, might even attract the death penalty but, even in biblical times was most difficult to prove. Same sex marriage in Israel is not permitted so that two people who want to get married have to go, for example, to Cyprus. When they return to Israel, secular law takes over, and a married same sex couple will not be disturbed by rabbinic law.

The Catholic Church does not recognise or perform same sex marriage and they condemn all sexual activity outside marriage but they will permit a formal blessing to a same sex couple. This piece of intellectual jiggery pokery takes us into the realms of metaphysics where no logical mind can follow them. Cardinal Newman, on the other hand sublimated the feelings he had for Ambrose St John who never allowed his deep and lasting friendship to become anything more, or less than that; a long friendship.

Islam has always condemned any homosexual activity but without asking for the death penalty or any record of it being a capital offence other than, possibly, in the Hadith, which is a record of what the Prophet is remembered to have said but not written. The Global Alliance for LGBT Education (GALE) has recorded some thirteen highly condemnatory statements from the Quran which cause the writer disgust without calling for the death penalty. Nevertheless, several Islamic countries impose the death sentence for homosexuality. This can have nothing to do with the faith itself but more with the poverty of the people who live in those states. Loosely speaking, they are failed states and it is convenient for their governments to have one or more scapegoats in much the same way as the Russian Tsars used the Jews and allowed and even encouraged the pogroms in which hundreds of Jews were murdered in various localities in Russia. As Russia became poorer, the pogroms got worse until the pain of poverty could no longer be alleviated by anti-Semitism and vented itself in revolution.

The truth is much more prosaic and has nothing to do with divine will. Anthony Bogaert, the Canadian psychologist, in the last 10 years, came up with what was then a theory: the more older brothers a person has, the more likely he is to be homosexual. This seems to be true and one might speculate that it is based on the amount of testosterone the mother bestows on the foetus. With later births, the amount of testosterone available dwindles and the chances of homosexuality increase. He also proposes a third form of sexuality-asexuality in which the person feels nothing or very little for either sex. This might also describe a state caused by shame which Freud called narcissism. The effect of shame is to do the individual shamed great damage in the first instance.

In the thoughtful film 'Shame', the symptoms of shame are examined. The protagonist can form no human relationship whatever. He can only pay prostitutes for sex. He masturbates regularly but when a pretty girl offers to fall in love with him, he is impotent. His sister is prepared to allow herself to be used as a chattel for passing men in spite of being a talented singer, until she attempts suicide and that might be a turning point in their lives except for his mother who continues to make her weekly phone call telling him she is dying and has only a week to live. When is she going to hear from him? All the characters in the film, which is a great social document, have internalised their shame and are damaging only themselves and their immediate families. They have yet to project their shame on to someone else when the real damage will begin, if they ever do .

There is considerable evidence in Bogaert's book 'Asexuality' for saying we are all bisexual though at various times, in every life, homosexuality or heterosexuality is in the ascendancy. Layla Moran, the liberal politician, did a great service to society by saying she was pan-sexual which seemed to mean that she would sleep with anyone to whom she took a liking. Bogaert maintains that this is not at all unusual in a serial manner. After all, logic indicates that we could not have same-sex friends unless we were, to some extent, bi sexual. With friends there might be never any physical connection other than a hand shake. The idea that humans are all, to some extent, bisexual provides an explanation for same sex friendship (you judge a man by his friends) but also the intense comradeship which exists when people are required to face danger together (Simmels rule). Many thousands of years ago, women banded together when they had to face a common enemy in the shape of men who were considered superior to women probably because of their greater physical strength and earning power. With earning power spread more evenly, all that has disappeared but it is dying hard and there is so much resentment from men they know that women are still being murdered at the rate of two per week in the UK.

The smallest social unit in the UK is the family and they are linked together by common memories. The memory is seated in the hypothalamus, part of the limbic system, so that common memories might well generate common emotions, whether good or bad, happy or sad. One of the most powerful common forces is having shared a common experience like both, or all , having been in the army, at the same university or sharing a common prejudice such as hating another ethnic group. In times of difficulty whether war or recession, it is a help to recall the heroes of an earlier period such as Elizabeth Tudor and the defeat of the Spanish Armada in 1588. There is no mention of the Spanish blunder in not landing a force in Plymouth in the calm before the storm. The myth has always been maintained that English sea dogs won the battle. The subsequent storm, when it blew up, was crucial in wrecking the Spanish fleet and made it impossible to pick up the army in the Spanish Netherlands. Queen Elizabeth herself gave birth to the myth of gallant seamanship in a letter to a friend, in which she emphasised that her body was that of a frail woman but her heart was that of a king and a king of England no less, as though wishing she had led her fleet into battle as kings had been required to in her recent past. The truth seems to be that the weather had more to do with the defeat of the Armada than any other single factor though the English ships had a greater rate of fire thanks to modifications made by Hawkins. The sharing of these sort of myths are what makes a nation though they are frequently no more than a version of the truth. She accepted the accolade of the 'Virgin Queen' which had overtones of the great virgin mother enshrined in Christianity as The Virgin Mary, mother of Jesus. Nothing could have been further from the truth as Elizabeth enjoyed quite an active sex life and her name is associated with the Earl of Leicester; Sir Christopher Hatton and Walter Raleigh. She was said to have had a number pregnancies as a result of her liaison with the Earl of Leicester.[26] She was a great

---

[26] Louis Montrose: The Subject of Elizabeth pp.125, 127, 202.

monarch and not being burdened with celibacy must have been a help.

The battle of Waterloo was won by a consortium of European nations, the seventh such consortium William Pitt had cobbled together. Famously, it was the arrival of Blucher, an Austrian, at the head of a Prussian army, out of the woods on Marshal Ney's right flank which swung the day. The one man who deserves his place in history from that period is Admiral Nelson, no relative, a magnificent seaman who had been at sea from the age of twelve. His mistress, Lady Hamilton, was devoted to him and personally cut up his meat for him when they were together, he having lost an arm in battle. She understood him having been a pretty, kept woman most of her life though honoured in battle in her own right. She was no physical coward and she understood men. The role of the more experienced woman in the lives of men closer to the middle of the spectrum of bisexuality has not been explored except, possibly, in Colette's novels Cherie and The Last of Cherie. Aged 19 Cherie has a long affair with a 49 year old demi mondaine called Léa, friend of his mother, which lasts six years. He marries, goes into the army to serve in World War I. He is away for six years and finds, on his return, that his wife is quite happy without him and, indeed, without marriage. He goes to see Léa to find she is grossly overweight with her head covered in grey stubble. The woman he loves is still alive but gone, both at the same time. Gazing at photographs of the woman he loves, the young Léa, he takes out his revolver and takes his own life. The novel is about where, on the sexuality spectrum, the main characters are situated.

As has already been observed, people have, more than a norm, more an instinct, a preference for those who look like them. This syndrome might well be related to fertility and to common memory and myth loyalty. Cousins have more children and those with common memories are more loyal because, in a white society anyone who fails to comply with the stereotype, the image which English people have of themselves, is made to feel inadequate in proportion to their departure from the so-called 'perfect norm' providing always that they have internalised it. Based purely on the behaviour which can be seen on television at the present time, the newsreaders have mainly white skin and lightened hair, light coloured eyes, preferably blue. Examined with care, a list of broadcasters in factual television, available to give talks (for a fee) contained some well known faces and numbered 109 from one agency and could be categorised as follows:

High Lighted Hair	30
Dark skin	15
Women	50
Men	59

In order to provide some contrast, another agency was offering after dinner speakers (for a fee) from among sports commentators. This also contained some well known faces:

High Lighted Hair	7
Dark Skin	5
Women	13
Men	40

Both these agencies had taken on clients they thought they could sell for a fee. For them, they were not engaged in a moral crusade but the sports followers showed a marked preference for white males, people who looked like them. The marked difference between the two lists is the drop in dark skinned people on offer. Those following sport were not prepared to depart too far from accepting someone who talked like them and looked like them. Whether men or women, the spectators are, on the whole not prepared to sit down and listen, with respect, to someone on account of the colour of their skin and/or their gender. Nor, possibly, laugh at their jokes. To do so would be to treat them as equals and to do so would be to lower themselves in their own estimation. The BBC are doing a stalwart job in educating the population into looking at the the human being and not judge them by their appearance. The author recalls lower middle class people in the 1960s displaying anguish and shame because black immigrants were moving into their street. Such people were among those who found themselves in a financial decline and unable to maintain their lifestyle. The people who voted for Brexit were not of any particular class but simply people of any class who were under threat of being unable to maintain their lifestyle[27] or, more importantly to attain the lifestyle expectations they and their parents expected of them. It was a most acute observation to argue Brexit, the leaving of the European trade bloc, on the basis that it was being run by foreigners who were making a fortune out of us and plastering slogans to that effect on the outside of hired London bus, a double decker of an older style as though as to say:'Let us get back to our traditional values.' The bus promised the viewer a sum of money weekly to be devoted to the NHS. With the decline of religion, many people look

---

[27] Lorenza Antonucci et al Brexit was not the voice of the working class LSE

upon the National Health Service as a sort of substitute which will extend their life on earth. Which to be fair, it tries to do. The sum of money promised has never materialised was economical with the truth from the beginning. But it was clever because arguing to remain within the European Union was arguing against the poor having a prosperous, extended life. Such people were viewed as 'The Enemy' by some very decent people but Jo Cox paid with her life. Those whose way of life is threatened are those who are most likely to vote for the status ante in the hope they will drift back to the way things were when they were younger. It goes without saying that it never does. Sad people were heard saying: 'I want my country/life back'.

The most obvious factor which makes people feel their way of life is threatened is a downturn in the economy. The bank crash of 2008 was due to American banks investing in worthless property for which there was no real underlying value when money became tight and the occupants were no longer able to pay their mortgages. Governments all over the Western world propped up the failing banks by filling the holes in their balance sheets left by having to write off the worthless properties with digital money. Banks became over cautious in lending money and when Lehman Brothers were allowed to fail, banks further afield than the United States became thoroughly alarmed and reined in lending. Britain, for one, went into recession and never really came out of it possibly because the then government stuck to nothing more enterprising than quantitative easing. (The purchase by the Bank of England of its own unsold gilts.) The previous great recession had been cured in America by printing money to pay for a massive increase in public works. Such a policy might have had it's difficulties because membership of the European Union would have sucked in more labour unless similar policies were employed by other nations within the Union. The UK continued with austerity and unemployment rose until some 20% of UK households were without work.

For reasons which have been touched upon frequently here there is a norm which says the measure of poverty is a measure of failure. Unfortunately for this particular norm, it is not a measure of failure of the individual but a failure of government. The most numerous in any society are the poor and it is the poor who are looked down upon in a society which admires money and respects the rich. Michael Stemley, in his book Wealth Power Respect says at p.4:

'I'm not a financial wizard or guru but I taught myself about wealth, the power it has and the respect that comes along with it...'[28]

What is absolutely clear is that we all respect soundly invested wealth and the more intelligent are suspicious of anything at all flashy. He points out the difference between capital investment and wasting assets. A capital asset is an insured house that one can afford to replace and a wasting asset is a motorcar which will one day be worthless though all need increasing maintenance. Too much of one's income spent on

---

[28]   Stemley is black and comes from New Orleans. He is writing about how wealth could protect the individual against life's hurricanes if, or when, they come along.

58

wasting assets is considered 'flashy'. In England, one of the little conceits which still exist is that old money is better than new money and almost derelict old men will mention that they have a member of the squirearchy or, or better still, a member of the aristocracy in their family. This sad form of boasting should be treated, where possible, with kindness.

In our society the measure of success is based on how great an income does an individual enjoy. In the popular mind, there are two measures of acceptability: one is income, the other is how close to the imaginary stereotype does he or she look. On that basis the bottom of the hierarchy are poor blacks and poor Jews though for different reasons. This is borne out in practice by a woman in Los Angeles writing in 2005 who was good enough to post her prejudices on the web as follows starting from what she considered to be the top:

English – German – French – North West European mixtures – Spanish or Portuguese – multiracial South and East European mixtures – Italians – other eastern or southern Europeans – Irish – multi-ethnic half white "good Asian" and "white tribe native American" – multiracial mixed with dark skin people – multiracial half white with light-skinned people – Asians, Chinese Japanese Vietnamese Korean, other good light skinned Asians – Multiracial, less than half, black with any other race providing they were light-skinned – multiracial of mixed heritage with not more than half black, brown skin – Pacific island – all other Native American – African northern or eastern and light-skinned – Middle Eastern, Iraqis, Arabs – Sephardic Jews from Spain Italy and South Europe – any other Jews with darker skin – Russian Jews – Ethiopian Jews – Ethiopian Somalis – blacks from Africa and those in the African Diaspora – black African Americans, descendants of slaves.

This is a remarkably detailed list which seems to be based on her idea of skin colour and when they might have appeared in the US, though Native Americans appear toward the bottom of the list. Education is not mentioned possibly because she herself is uneducated. Appearance is all. Ex President Obama being interviewed by David Olusoga on the BBC in November 2020 said much the same: that they, those with white skin, look down on people who do not look like them. Appearance, when combined with shame forms a lethal mix whether the shame is based on poverty or on some form of sexuality which their religion does not approve of. These, seem to be the main sources of shame.

The practice of many people to base their opinions on appearance and little more is so strong that in England many people are judged, to a large extent, by their possessions. This is true, in particular, for cars and houses which are visible and some pauper themselves to keep up with their peer group having failed to maintain the privileges of the society they were born in to. The infamous case of John Bingham, the 7th Earl of Lucan (1934 up to his disappearance in 1974), was apparently such an occurrence- an attempt to restore his fortunes by murder. While those who fail to keep up with their peer group earn contempt, those who, because of real poverty, have to rely, in whole or in part, on state aid are regarded by many with contempt and are not accepted as equals by the society they live in. In any society, not being accepted can give rise to violence. In England, as has been noted repeatedly, it is appearance and speech which make you 'one of us'. This makes it very difficult for people with black skin to feel they belong and some switch to another group who have also been vilified and where they can feel they do belong. Belongingness is the basic psychological need of any individual according to Maslow[29]. Black people who are made to feel they do not belong turn to a group where they do belong and, at the present time, they sometimes turn to Islam. Those that do so, behave in a particularly zealous manner. This was so in the case of the two men who murdered Lee Rigby, an off duty soldier. The pair refrained from hurting civilians. They were not going behave as the British army had done in Iraq[30]. This latter sentiment is unfair and inaccurate. The army is there to carry out the will of parliament. The error, if any, lay in parliament voting for war.

Shame is an essential first step in that a person, who feels shame, will display prejudice against someone who is lower down the stereotypical chain than they are.   Shame, it is alleged here, is a first step in bullying. Thus, someone who is poorer than their peers, though having white skin, will gain relief from their shame by refusing to live with, or near, someone with black skin or refuse to accept a Jew or a homosexual as an equal.   Inner shame when talking to

---

[29]   Abraham Maslow 1908-1970 Professor of Psychology at three places of learning, finally at Brandeis University.
[30]   It was the American policy of Shock and Awe that many found distasteful and ruined the reputation of the Labour Party.

someone closer to the ideal stereotype is sometimes shown by gaze aversion, brief mental confusion and a longing to disappear, usually accompanied by blushing of the face, neck or chest.[31] The shame spectrum set out by Dr Burgo are all painful experiences in the face of criticism from those around. In other words, not being accepted by the society a human lives in because they look different or being looked down on because of having failed to measure up to the accepted standards of the immediate society the victim lives in is a source of shame. The capacity to experience shame stems from surviving in small primitive societies over many thousands of years when, to be ostracised or declared an outlaw could mean death from starvation. As Maslow observed, the failure to be accepted and belong to a group is damaging to the individual. It is important to note that shame is imposed by the group or the society the shamed victim lives in and upon which he relies on to stay alive.

In summary, as has been recognised above, there are various categories under which perfectly worthy people are looked down upon. Poverty displayed in clothing; homosexuality sometimes displayed in mannerisms; and darker skin. Colossal sums of money are spent in many affluent societies around the world trying to look like a stereotype with paler skin, smarter clothing and supporting winning teams. People who are unable or disinclined to conform with what is considered the ideal are sometimes subjected to put downs in the 'affluent society' and their solution is to bolster their feelings of self by boosting their self esteem by bullying someone who has themselves been vilified.

---

[31] Dr J Burgo: 'Shame' Loc 88

The main reactions to shame are to internalise it but remain in every respect the same and give way to those who are accepted members of the native population and allow them to make snide remarks and even cast insults and humiliation. This behaviour is more painful if done in public, like being put in the stocks.

The next is to hit back at the native group by boasting about achievements that place one closer to the native hierarchy such as assuming an anglo-saxon name as the royal family did during WW1, abandoning the German: Saxe-Coburg-Gotha and assuming the name Windsor.

More aggressive are the plays of Tennessee Williams, a homosexual. In Suddenly Last Summer he depicts the genteel Southern society which condemns him for what he is. They are shown to be rotten, taking advantage of poor children for sexual purposes and using wealth obtained from Slavery to buy obedience.

Finally there are those of a different appearance who are humiliated on a daily basis and run amok on London Bridge, killing indiscriminately. This latter class always, tragically, wreak their vengeance on the innocent before the police shoot them. They sometimes wear a suicide vest to ensure the police do end their lives.

Lastly there are those who make a success of their lives and rise above any attempt at humiliation responding to any attempt at abuse or humiliation with silence, or a faux pretence of not understanding or, best of all, a bright, friendly smile.

Section 5: Populism

Adolf Hitler, Donald Trump, The Conservative Party, The Pogroms in Russia, Social Banditry

Populism is the practice of blaming the present privations, whatever they may be, providing they are widespread so that many project their shame on to people who do not look like 'us' and/or speak like 'us'. It follows then, that populism has it's greatest effect when people, of whatever position in society, feel their way of life is threatened. Usually economically, they project their shame on to what they think of as 'foreigners'. Populism follows Simmel's Law, discussed earlier, which says a group is bound together when facing a common enemy.

In the last 1,000 years, since Christianity arrived in Rome, the scapegoat of preference was the Jew but in more recent times, since the arrival of immigrant labour to man the factories of Lancashire, there has tended to be a preference for the scapegoat to be the 'Muslim'. The difference between the two is interesting: The denigration of Jews is based on propaganda which reduces normal empathy whereas the denigration of Muslims is based on appearance and is closer

64

to primitive tribal loyalty and recognition of the 'enemy'. The politician who gets it right and expresses distaste for the locally denigrated group will get that local group vote.

The evil Muslim was created in the US by Osama bin Laden who sent suicide bombers to hijack four airliners and crash them into chosen targets. Two of them hit the twin towers in New York, one hit the Pentagon and one was brought down by the passengers who sacrificed their own lives to save others as it was heading for Washington. Nearly 3,000 lives were lost, all innocent. The populist politician sneers and makes jokes about the target population even though he knows perfectly well they may have never heard of Osama bin Laden or had nothing to do with the death of the Christian Saviour to show they too are one of the threatened group. If the group who feels themselves threatened is large enough, the populist politician will get elected.

During economic slumps when jobs are hard to find, human beings go back to some period when they were tribal subsistence farmers and their very existence depended on feeding their women and children so that the human race could continue. Their very existence is thus threatened and they project this threat on to an alien group who do not look like them and who do not talk like them. These people are the enemy and any politician who joins them in fighting against such a group is a comrade in arms, and will get their vote This, unlikely as it sounds in the modern, Western world is the emotional reasoning that comes to the fore and controls the way we vote. Nor is this a recent syndrome:

Edmund Burke (1723-1792) said to his electorate in Bristol

> *'If I no longer give you the benefit of my judgement and
> simply follow your orders, I am not serving you; I am
> betraying you.'*[32]

For those with low integrity this route to easy success is
irresistible but for those who have been taught to to think
rationally, the cortex eventually takes over after mature
thought but until then, the limbic system holds sway and we
reason emotionally. For most, it is patchy. Some problems
are considered rationally while others are subject to the
emotions.

In the aftermath of a war, when infrastructure has been
destroyed and economic systems have come under attack that
racism and the populism that needs it to succeed, come to
the fore. Cheap politicians get votes during a recession or,
better still from their point of view, a slump. They use some
form of populism described above and make sneering
remarks about some minority group.

Adolf Hitler

The arch populist of modern times was Adolf Hitler(1889-
1945), the dictator of Germany. Christianity had preached
for 1,000 years, since it took power in Rome, that the Jews
had murdered the Christian saviour so that people all over
Europe were prepared to understand that the people who
stood ready to jeopardise their way of life were the Jews.

---

[32] Andrew Ryder, Britain and Europe at a Crossroads p.76

The German people in particular had been prepared to think in this way by the humiliation of losing WWI. The origins of WWI are obscure. The Germans felt they were losing out in the race for empire. They had had an easy victory in the Franco Prussian War of 1870 and made the French pay compensation which, it is interesting to note, produced inflation in Berlin and a surge of already existing anti Semitism in France which gave rise to the immensely successful La France Juive, a fiercely anti Jewish book, which was published in 1886 and went on for many more editions. It's purpose and effect was to give the French someone to look down on thus bolstering their self esteem and giving them a feeling of control, a very common need for those defeated in battle. It spawned similar publications across Europe. Such is the futility of war. Neither victor nor vanquished gain anything from it and many times both sides come out of it poorer and an innocent third party comes out of it even worse off than he was before. The character of the victorious general is magnified to being a military genius like General Rommel in North Africa in WW II. Similarly General Zhukov also in WW II. Both men had to be removed by their respective dictators: Rommel to his death and Zhukov to Siberia.

After the Franco Prussian war, the German military came up with the Schlieffen plan designed to conquer the French and take Paris, together with anyone else who intervened, in six weeks.   The plan was put on the back burner for decades. It was totally illegal, involving the surprise invasion of Belgium then swinging West and taking Paris, whereupon, it was supposed, the French would capitulate and the German army would then be free to travel East and deal with Russia. The plan was infantile and the Kaiser was reluctant to get involved in such a risky enterprise. His mother was the British Princess Royal and there was a possibility the UK would come in on the side of the French bringing her vast Empire with her. On the other hand Germany had been united by Bismark under Prussia and a Prussian king so that they thought of themselves as much stronger than they were in 1870. All the other provinces of Germany had to send an Embassy together with an ambassador to Berlin. Von Moltke revamped the Plan and persuaded the Kaiser to launch an attack to avoid being surrounded by British power, including sea power.

In 1914 Germany declared war and the British Expeditionary Force stood between the German army and Paris. The courage and resolution shown by both sides brings tears to the sensitive reader's eyes. The war became a siege which could only be resolved, in the opinion of British historians like Lord Wavell, by a siege machine or starvation. All the military opted for 'the break through' and tens of thousands died attacking fixed machine guns and artillery in order to pierce fixed enemy lines.

The Plan lay in the dust and von Moltke retired to his country estate in Brandenberg and had a stroke; leaving Europe to the most bloody conflict it had ever experienced. Finally the RNVR long range blockade of North Sea ports starved the Germans into submission and German families were writing to their men at the front begging them to stop the war. Quite suddenly large numbers of German soldiers capitulated

68

together with their officers in1918. This became known as 'the stab in the back' and it was somehow attributed to the Jews who were accused of betraying the honour of Germany.

There then began a series of humiliations starting with the Versailles agreement headed by the Americans which was viewed by the Germans as nothing more than a military diktat imposed upon the vanquished by the victors. It laid down reparations which Germany was to pay to the entente powers which, incidently, the Germans seem never to have paid. Hindenburg remained president and sent the Kaiser into exile in Holland to act as the scapegoat for the loss of the war. The Chancellor, Muller, seems to have continued with certain welfare practices: unemployment benefit and certain state pensions. In 1923, the French with some 60,000 soldiers occupied the Ruhr in search of their reparations and the German workers, as instructed, went on strike. Germany printed money to keep the country going but without the Ruhr, and unemployment benefit, the country was bankrupt.

Two events then took place: A brilliantly clever man called Hjalmar Schacht invented a new currency, the Rentenmark, which, unencumbered with benefits and pensions coupled with the departure of the French from the Ruhr, soon became a stable currency; secondly, the absence of any stable currency had given rise to unemployment and criminality as everything was up for sale and every kind of prostitution was available in which every kind of sexuality was catered for. In order to restore some sort of order, Reichschancellor Bruning called in unemployed soldiers from the German army to form a vigilante force to beat up malefactors as they saw fit. Rosa Luxemburg and Karl Liebknecht of the Red Flag were murdered with their bodies dumped by the side of a road. People all over Germany were in a state of misery and suspected the Jews who had murdered the Christian saviour were to blame for their misery. This view was reinforced by the Nazi party whose paper, Der Sturmer, showed grotesque caricatures of Jews using their wealth to despoil fair haired German maidens. This established in the minds of the German people that Jews did not look like them and did not behave like them. Unemployment and prejudice brought the Nazi Party to power in 1933, nominally led by Adolf Hitler.

Hitler was chosen to lead the Nazi Party, possibly by Goering, because he most closely resembled their electorate. He had been a non commissioned soldier in WWI like them. He came from a poor background and he had won the Iron Cross for bravery which was certainly admirable. Whilst not being 'Aryan', he had black hair, he did have blue eyes which flickered interestingly when he spoke. He was a riveting speaker who was going to deal with the Jews and the Communists and make Germany great again. This was what Germans wanted to hear from a leader and so they voted for him. He seems to have been devoid of subtlety or intelligence. He was a bully and within 12 years Germany was a smoking ruin. At his trial in Nuremburg, Goering seemed unaware that he was on trial for genocide and merely remarked, quite correctly, that the Nazi Party had not invented anti Semitism. He was found guilty but took a cyanide tablet before the hangman could get at him.

Nevertheless what he said was true and guilt for the holocaust should be shared with the German people.

Donald Trump

The next individual who rose to great power with the battle cry that he was going to make America great again was President Donald Trump who was in office from January 2017 to January 2021 when he was declared the loser of the election of 2020 and Joe Biden was sworn in as President. The terrible events of 2001 organised by Osama bin Laden when 19 suicide bombers hi-jacked American airliners and crashed them into the twin towers in New York and the Pentagon. Osama bin Laden himself was a Saudi but a lot of oil was bought from them so that they were not condemned. Most of the hi-jackers were Egyptian and Egypt was one of the few allies the West had in the Middle East and so President Bush settled on Islam which he said meant 'peace' and tried not to be inflammatory, the rest of America referred to the killers as Muslims. Unfortunately this appellation ostracised millions of perfectly innocent people all over the world and blurred foreign policy decisions to the extent it finally led to the invasion of Afghanistan and a conflict with an empire of pashto speaking people who stretched from Iran to the head of the Indus basin. The next event which led to the triumph of populism was the bank crash of 2008 caused a stagnation of the US economy and a rise in unemployment which peaked in 2010 to 2011 at nearly 10% as banks all over the world were more careful about making loans in order to replenish their balance sheets. This was enough to bring an Islamophobe to power because in the minds of substantial numbers of ordinary people, the threat to their way of life was caused by 'the Muslim'. Hitler had used 'the Jew' and Trump used 'the Muslim'. Trump flogged 'the Muslim' invective to such an extent that most decent people tired of it.

The Washington Post published a book: Donald Trump and his Assault on TRUTH too voluminous to quote in full but here are some early extracts:

> *"Donald Trump, the most mendacious president in US history. He almost never expresses regret. He is not known for one big lie-just a constant stream of exaggerated, invented, boastful, purposely outrageous, spiteful, inconsistent, dubious and false claims."*

One hallmark of Trump's dishonesty is that if he thinks of false or incorrect claim is a winner, he will repeat it constantly no matter how often it has been proven wrong. Many politicians are embarrassed to receive a four Pinocchio rating; often, they will drop all and refine the offending talking point. Some even apologise for their departure from the truth. Trump digs in and doubles down. He keeps going long after the facts are clear, in what appears to be a deliberate effort to replace the truth with his own, far more favourable, version.

Trump claimed that the Uzbekistan-born man who in 2017 was accused of killing eight people with a pickup truck in New York had brought two dozen relatives to the United States through social chain migration. In actual fact he had brought none.

> "Mexico's paying for the wall. You know that. You'll see that. It's all worked out. Mexico's paying."

Trump first made this promise when he announced his candidacy in June 2015.

> "I would build a great wall, and nobody builds walls better than me, believe me," he told the crowd. "I'll build them very inexpensively, I will build a great, great wall on our southern border. And I will have Mexico pay for that wall"

Mexico has not paid for the wall. Nor is there any suggestion that it will. A leaked transcript from Trump's first weeks in office suggests even he wasn't convinced that Mexico would pay.

'Nov.16, 2015: Following a series of terrorist attacks in Paris, Trump said on MSNBC that he would,

> "Strongly consider closing mosques. I would hate to do it, but it's something you're going to have to strongly consider because some of the ideas and some of the hatred, the absolute hatred, is coming from these areas."

He also tried misogyny with Mrs Clinton, on one occasion, following close behind her, his huge bulk towering over her as she moved around the stage. She glanced behind her and just smiled.

Nevertheless, in spite of, or because of, this behaviour, he won the election because he rightly judged that his voters were women hater, xenophobes. In fact he went to considerable pains, according to a BBC documentary, to have people listening in to social media to enable him to tell people what they wanted to hear.

Unemployment continued to decline until the pandemic of 2019 when he failed to respond with sufficient vigour, went into denial that the situation was so bad, many died and he lost the election to Mr Biden. Unemployment rocketed until the peak of the pandemic passed. The populist who gives a tribal message to people who want to hear it because it fulfils their emotional needs as they struggle to maintain their way of life will always get their vote regardless of the candidate's lack of ability. The Trump administration approved a pipeline in the Arctic in spite of the Secretary of State a former CEO of Exxon Mobil recusing himself at the insistence of Greenpeace. Telling lies is part of the populist game because people are so pleased to hear what they want to hear that they do not want to check the statement. We all want to hear the 'enemy' is losing.

The Conservative Party

In the UK, the economy and employment played it's part in threatening the life style of millions of people but it was not as conclusive as in the US. The determination with which the UK pursued austerity instead of expanding the economy by printing money for investment projects went as follows: 2009, 200 billion; 2012, 375 billion; 2016, 445 billion; 2020, 645 billion; 2020 745 billion; 2021 895 billion. The acceleration in the money supply in 2020-2021 is an indication of the arrival of a new Chancellor keeping the economy moving during the Covid 19 pandemic. The printing of this amount of money cannot continue because leaving the European Union together with restrictions on travel due to the pandemic has taken any slack out of the economy so that in order to invest, taxes have had to be raised. This is a creditable performance by a man (Mr Sunak) who comes from a section of the population vilified by Mr Johnson, the PM. Mr Johnson in order to gain power in the 2019 election made jokes about the clothes immigrant women wore. For the purposes of tracing the rise of the next populist, Mr Johnson, the vilification of those who did not speak English as their native tongue, particularly those with dark skin carried him to power and out of Europe.

Immigration from the colonies began in earnest after the war in 1947 when sailors from Pakistan began settling and finding work in the UK. Many more from the Indian subcontinent were invited in as cheap labour for the textile industry and settled in Lancashire, Yorkshire, in particular, Bradford. There was a further influx to the West Midlands as the motor industry faced competition from Japan and Europe. British manufacturers providing vehicles for a mass market have now virtually disappeared though some of the names, now foreign owned, are still extant. A number of these immigrants, those who came from Pakistan and Bangladesh, were Muslim by faith and 'Muslim' became shorthand for any immigrant with dark skin. Britain, in particular England, was prospering as a member of the

European Union but the prosperity was not evenly spread and some areas, namely the North East, the Midlands and Wales there were areas of severe poverty[33] Mr Cameron, the then prime minister, delivered an anti immigrant speech at the University of Suffolk 25 March 2015 saying that immigration had to be controlled because that was the reasonable thing to do and Mrs May, then home secretary, was of the same opinion. The press gave a lot of attention to a man called Abu Hamza who preached against Britain, had a hook, had lost an eye, lived on benefits and became, in the popular mind, the arch immigrant and the delay in extraditing him helped swing the Brexit vote in favour of leaving the EU.

For those in poverty the route to Brexit was simple; it consisted almost entirely in repeating again and again that the Europeans permitted uncontrolled immigration. The fact that the EU free movement of labour enshrined in the Maastricht agreement applied to Europeans only was lost on the electorate of 2016 and they continued to vote to exclude 'Muslims'. It was true that many human beings had been displaced in the wars in Iraq and Afghanistan instigated by the US in order to balance oil power and control Saddam Hussein but this instability would not be assuaged by leaving Europe, rather the contrary.

No party explained this to the voters and they voted to leave Europe under the impression that this would save them from immigration and make the country rich. This latter proposition was propagated by a large sum of money pasted on the side of a campaign bus occupied by Johnson, Gove and

---

[33] Andrew Ryder, Britain and Europe at a Crossroads p.76

Patel, all with hopes of taking high office. A poster of a line of Syrian refugees below the caption 'The EU has failed us. We must take control of our borders.' was followed by the murder of MP Jo Cox but anyone standing in the way of leaving was seen as an enemy standing in the way of the prosperity of getting out of the EU.. The British People voted to leave the EU 52% to 48%. Simmel's rule played a role and anyone standing in the way of the common enemy was a traitor.

The then Prime Minister, Cameron, resigned and Mrs May took his place. A rather more astute performer than her predecessor, she put the country back to work and unemployment fell. She negotiated a compromise withdrawal agreement with the EU, reduced unemployment to 3.74% and, had a further referendum been held, the UK would have remained. She presented her withdrawal bill on three occasions but each time it was rejected by her own party, the conservatives, and she resigned as she had to, there was no option. Mr Johnson took her place as leader and called an election. Not, it will be noted, a referendum. Had a referendum been called, because of the reduction in unemployment, it might have reversed the 2016 result and so the proponents of the status quo called for all to respect the will of the people even though the result of not calling a referendum might not be in the interests of the nation. The conservatives concentrated on the poor Midlands constituencies which had always been Labour but who had voted Leave in the referendum of 2016. Mr Johnson had previously prepared to take high office by saying:

Whatever happened this year in Andijan, when Karmov's troops slaughtered between 80 and 300 people, Islamic revivalism was there.

Whatever you say about the Russians, they have no qualms about abusing human rights, if that means cracking down on Islam.

Claimed that:

"12 serious attacks on Muslims in Britain in the space of four months does not speak of a climate of vicious reprisals."

Johnson compared Muslim women wearing the burqa to letter boxes, a remark for which he subsequently apologised.

The effect of these remarks was to instil in the minds of many that he was biased against anyone of a non-white appearance but in the minds of many more that he was their champion against a common enemy, the Muslim. So odious did many find his remarks that Suhaiymah Manzoor-Khan, writing in the Guardian (5 Jan 2020), said:

"Boris Johnson is one of the most openly racist and Islamophobic politicians in recent British history."

Johnson himself has said that he only made such remarks when he was a newspaper man and campaigning for office. Now that he has been elected Prime Minister, such remarks are inappropriate or unnecessary. The old saying that what is in his heart will one day come out of his mouth might apply and the Jury is still out on what sort of man he really is. The historic fact is that the Conservatives won the 2019 election with an increased majority. The Labour leader campaigned in a cloth cap and muffler, drank stout and masqueraded as a member of the Working Class. He was written off as patronising because the working class has now disappeared and everyone is a middle class house owner and such a stance alienated many former Labour voters.

While a narrative devoted to denigrating 'the Muslim' served to endear part of the population to the Brexit cause because it would stem the 'flood' of immigrants, no such flood actually appeared other than a few thousand homeless creatures who were camping in Calais. It has to be said that there was a flood pending because the Western world had destabilised the Middle East and the flow of the destitute who were being held up in Turkey and paid for by the EU, the very organisation the UK was trying to leave. There was another factor which was alienating the poor white and that was the increasing wealth of the Indian immigrant population who, by 2018 had overtaken the poor white skinned population.[34] There was another piece of demography which was never mentioned during the campaign was that Britain was in increasing need for immigrants to maintain the population. British born women of whatever appearance were now, thanks to birth control pills, in control of their own fertility. The fertility rate in 2020 was 1.57 children per woman which means there is a need for 200,000 to 300,000 immigrants per year to maintain the population.

---

[34] Joseph Rowntree Trust Working Age Employment Rate

All the logic was on the side of remaining. The leave campaign was based on a purely emotional argument that the UK was about to be submerged in immigrants. It is true that large numbers of refugees dislodged by US wars in the Middle East have been stopped in Turkey and the EU is providing a fund of €6,000 million of which the UK is helping with £68 million per annum. There are no winners in modern warfare.

The leave campaign prepared by the Conservative splinter group who failed to support Mrs May sounded as though they were living in the age of Empire which, though it did last for 300 years, by the 21st Century, was dead. This was misleading. What soon emerged was a completely different group who had stood behind Johnson's populism and now seem to have staged a coup. A meritocracy who did not rely on white appearance.

A majority of white, British politicians cried out that membership of the EU spelt the end of independent sovereignty but this was a sentimental illusion. The painful discovery that independent British sovereignty was a thing of the past came with the Suez crisis of 1956 when Egypt in the shape of Gamel Abdul Nasser nationalised the Suez Canal. The Canal had an almost mystical significance in the minds of right wing politicians as the route to the Empire Britain and France invaded the canal zone to protect it from the Israelis who were only pretending to invade to lend credence to this charade. The US, who had not been consulted, offered no support and there was a run on sterling which, had it been allowed to continue, would have brought the British economy into jeopardy.

Britain and France immediately withdrew. Thereafter the UK assisted the US in their foreign adventures under the slogan 'special relationship' though some Labour leaders, namely Harold Wilson and Gordon Brown were less ready to put the country at risk. In about 1960 President Kennedy asked Harold Macmillan to join the EEC or Common Market possibly because it would suit American interests to have a junior ally in Europe. President De Gaulle vetoed British entry. Entry would have also been in UK interests giving UK a home market the size of the US. The UK applied again and was vetoed by the same De Gaulle. The UK applied again in 1972 when De Gaulle had been deposed and was successful though never joined the Euro which left a considerable degree of independence.

For many in the country who also followed events, possibly not many in numbers, but a kind of intelligent elite. For them membership of the EEC was only just acceptable for trade purposes. Maastricht with what was seen as the beginnings of a European Super State with its own foreign policy and its own army was a step too far. Britain was losing independence and, hence, sovereignty. They found one of their number who was biddable and, using xenophobia, made him prime minister.

Johnson voiced this conviction at the Conservative national conference in 2019: 'This country has long been a pioneer. We inaugurated the steam age, the age of the genome. We led the way in parliamentary democracy, in female emancipation. And when the whole world had succumbed to a different fashion, this country and this party pioneered ideas of free markets and privatisation that spread across the planet. Every one of them was controversial, every one of them was difficult, but we have always had the courage to be original, to do things differently, and now we are about to take another giant step to do something no one thought we could do. To reboot our politics, to relaunch ourselves into the world, and to dedicate ourselves again to that simple proposition that we are here to serve the democratic will of the British people.'[35]

This is fine Shakespearean rhetoric but, like Shakespeare, it is fiction invented to please others. A more realistic picture is revealed in 'Britannia Unchained' Editor Kwasi Kwarteng and contributed to by presently serving cabinet ministers (Raab, Truss and Patel) which argued that Britain rewards laziness and British workers are the worst idlers in the world.[36] The book itself cannot be argued with, espousing, as it does, Keynesian economics and entrepreneurial skill but looking down on care of the poor. The people presently running the country seem to have great academic skill but leaving the EU together with the 'lock down' required to combat a pandemic, has left the country with a paucity of immigrants and the slack needed to make investments without causing inflation. On the other hand, the paucity of cheap labour caused the UK to invest into the high tech economy, a change, some would argue, UK should have made a couple of decades ago.

Having said all this, it cannot be said that Western leaders are devoid of physical courage. During the Russian attack on

---

[35]   Andrew Ryder p146
[36]   Andrew Ryder p.147

Ukraine, the leaders of Poland, Czech Republic and Slovenia visited Kyiv in March 2022 and the UK visited in April 2022. There is no record of Mr Putin visiting Ukraine since 2013.

The Pogroms in Russia

The Pogroms in Russia were adopted by the Okhrana to convince the Russian peasant population that the rising price of wheat was the fault of the Jews and, by killing Jews, the Tsarist government was doing something about it.

Russia had and still has, an unstable social structure with a massive peasantry being controlled, by a tiny aristocracy. Russian society has always lacked a middle class. One of the things that kept the serfs obedient was their belief in the ancient Slavic gods. Very few of the Russian peasantry had a church to go to until the 17th Century and they obeyed the gods who gave them fertility, a good crop and led them in battle in order to protect 'Damp Mother Earth' and who would never forgive someone who broke their word.[37] The one thing which bound them together was a common enemy in accordance with Simmel's Rule and that common enemy was 'The Jews' endowed on the Rus[38] at the end of the first Millennium when they adopted Christianity. Catherine the Great pushed the Jews into a huge area of land around the Baltic to colonise it with Russian speakers from 1772-1779 and after the First Partition of Poland. The area became

---

[37] Illustrated Encyclopedia of Ancient Slavic Gods and Spirits by Olga Kryuchkova et al.
[38] An early medieval people who gave their name to Russia.

known as the Pale of Settlement which included much of Ukraine. Russian populism was based on Jew hatred to rally the people behind the Tsar in a series of pogroms. Incidentally, the present dictator (Tsar) is trying to rally the people behind him with America hatred and a war to stop Ukraine falling into American hands.

Alexander II (1855-1881) saw that discontent was rising towards revolution and a safety valve had to be created, without which, there would be violence. He himself had had six attempts made on his life. He therefore instructed the landowners to sell some small part of their land to the serfs. This was complied with, with reluctance, and the worst land at high prices was put up for sale. Peasants broke their backs to pay for and own some land. Alexander became known as 'The Liberator'.

He was assassinated in 1881 by a member of the People's Will movement who did not want Alexander's tentative reforms to succeed. They wanted a complete collapse of the Tsarist government to alleviate the grim poverty that existed in the countryside, or so they thought. The peasants using their ancient survival mechanism, started to look for the enemy within who was occupying their land and came up with the Jews who spoke Yiddish to each other and had been wearing special clothing since 1835 by order of Nikolai I. They were therefore easily identifiable as foreigners in spite of having lived there for over 100 years. Far more important was that the Jews had been identified by the church as the killers of one of their gods, the Christian Saviour. Jesus had been added to the slavic pantheon progressively from about 540 CE in order to popularise the new religion. The Slavic gods regulated the normal scenario of gods required for the serfs to survive. Perun, usually the leading god, regulated the sacred tree, the oak, fertility, weapons, thunder and much more. Sventovid was a god of war, four headed with each head a different colour; it might be supposed that his function was to invade other lands and to defend the homeland. The Slavs were the most extensive ethnic group in the world stretching from the Baltic to Manchuria. They had hundreds of gods and Jesus was one of them. To kill a god was to threaten world order and in order to restore control, the killers had to be killed even if, curiously, they, as individuals, are innocent. Control of the environment one lives in is paramount. Without it, one could not exist.

The Odessa Pogrom 1859 was caused by instability in the price of wheat brought about by the aftermath of the Crimean war (1853-1856), the demand for wheat from the occupying armies and the disruption to farming in the Ukraine.[39] Jewish merchants who were prepared to operate at lower profit margins than the Greeks, prospered. It was said that they drove the Greek merchants out of business and preferred to employ fellow Jews. Whatever the true reason it must be clear that the Greek population suffered from higher levels of unemployment and they felt discriminated against. In addition the Christian Easter fell on April 24, the day that violence began when Christianity reminded its congregations that the Jews were guilty of

---

[39] Fischer, The Great Wave p.159

deicide. The Greek sailors who started the violence had had their reliance on shipping wheat disrupted by the war and the global trade in wheat, which had provided a solution to the bad winters between 1814 and 1818, had similarly been disrupted.

Russian society was inherently unstable with a very small middle class, an even smaller aristocracy who could be relied upon to be loyal to the Tsar under any circumstances. Beneath these two there was a huge population of serfs who were passive as long as they could believe that the Tsar expressed God's divine will on earth. There was the danger that this was shaken by Russia's defeat in the Crimea. By agreement with the land owners, the Tsar, Alexander II, proceeded with the emancipation of the serfs in which the landowners surrendered part of their land and kept two thirds for themselves. The land was divided into strips and each household had their strip. Unfortunately, they were sometimes too small to sustain a family. The state paid the landholders more than a fair price for the land they provided. Groups of serfs (communes) had to borrow on a mortgage from the state bank which they had to repay while they worked the land. They literally sweated blood to repay their loans[40] This, to a large extent, explains the Russian smallholder's resistance to Stalin's collectivisation plans after the Bolshevik Revolution. They were moved off their land in cattle trucks.

After the Crimean War the price of agricultural produce in

---

[40]   Macrohistory Alexander II More Reform and Economic Growth

Russia increased fivefold whilst the average industrial wage dropped 9%. By 1913 and the outbreak of the First World War the price of agricultural produce had gone up 600% whilst wages had increased by only 55%. By 1917 and the Bolshevik Revolution, prices had increased 700% at a time when wages had increased by 160%.[41] The Russian people were starving. The agricultural industry was being exposed to globalisation and surplus wheat was being exported to a world market which paid in hard currency. The chain which implemented this process was the land owners, the Greek grain merchants and the Jewish grain dealers. Clearly, racial prejudice ruled out the Russian land owners and the Greeks who were fellow Orthodox Christians could be ruled out also. This left the Jews, who were readily acceptable, in the popular mind, to be blamed for the hunger and poverty they were suffering. In a series of attacks they murdered Jews who had no connection with food.

In order to reinforce the suffering described in numbers above it is worth stating how little the wage would buy. The unskilled Russian labourer in the employ of the government might have been typical of the amount earned by the serfs. He was paid 10 kopeks per day which would have bought, very approximately, 14,000 calories of bread or potatoes. This unhealthy diet might have been enough to feed him and a family of four but with no surplus. It was a subsistence diet.

---

[41] AG Vinogradov National Economy of Russia and USSR 1515-2015 Loc 23682 for prices and Loc 14541 for wages using 1852 as the basis for comparison.

There were a series of pogroms, some in Odessa, which gradually became more and more serious and in which more and more Jews were killed. They took place in 1859, 1871 and from 1881 to 1906 on a regular annual basis. The 1905 pogrom, in Odessa, was the worst anti-Jewish pogrom in the sequence when over 400 Jews were killed. The pogroms nearly always occurred around Easter when the Christian communities were reminded in the churches that the Jews had caused the death of Jesus Christ. Many priests repeated the words in Thessalonians that, without qualification, the Jews had killed Christ. They did not mince their words.[42] The Russia authorities slowly realised that the pogroms provided an outlet for the discontent in the Russian community and the Bolshevik, Piatnitski, commenting on the 1905 pogrom, said that he recalled seeing gangs of young men between 25 and 30 years old who were rounding up anyone on the streets who looked like a Jew, stripping them naked and beating them mercilessly. The Bolsheviks fired at them and they ran away but at that moment a wall of soldiers appeared to protect the pogromists. This happened several times. It became clear to the Bolsheviks that the pogromists and the military were acting together[43]. The pogrom therefore was adopted by the Russian authority to give the illusion, in times of increasing economic distress, that the authorities were taking control and remedying the problem because the hated Jew who had killed the Saviour was the cause of the people's

---

[42]   That the Jews Killed the Christian Saviour is stated many times in the Gospels notably 1Thessalonians 2.14-16. The number of Jews who died is an estimate that comes from David Hackett Fischer's The Great Wave p.101
[43]   Wikipedia Odessa Pogroms

distress.   As always, it gives an illusion of control to find and kill the people responsible for the unhappiness you are suffering. The more foreign and weaker they are, the more convincing the solution.

Mark Twain leaves his readers in no doubt that the massacre of Jews in Bialystok in 1906 was provoked by Christian dogma and carried out on the orders of the government and their soldiery. He gives the following account:

> "Horrible details have been sent out by the correspondent of the Bourse Gazette who arrived in Bialystok in company with deputy Shepkin on Saturday, and who managed to send his story by a messenger Sunday afternoon. The correspondent, who accompanied Shepkin directly to the hospital escorted by a corporal's guard, says he was utterly unnerved by the sights he witnessed there."

"Merely saying that the bodies were mutilated," the correspondent writes, "fails to describe the awful facts. The faces of the dead have lost all human resemblance. The body of teacher Apstein lay on the grass with the hands tied. In the face and eyes had been hammered 3 inch nails. Rioters entered his home, killing him thus, and then murdered the rest of his family of seven. When the body arrived at the hospital it was also marked with a bayonet thrusts."

"Beside the body of Apstein lay that of a child of 10 years, whose leg had been chopped off with an axe. Here also lie the dead from the Schlachter home, where according to *witnesses, soldiers came and plundered the house and killed the wife, son, and neighbour's daughter and seriously wounded Schlachter and his two daughters."*

"I am told that soldiers entered the apartments of the Lapidus brothers which were crowded with people who had fled from the streets for safety, and ordered the Christians to separate themselves from the Jews. A Christian student named Dikar protested and was killed on the spot. Then all the Jews were shot"

There is the account of a badly wounded merchant named Nevyazhiky:

> *I live in the suburbs. Learning of the pogroms I tried to reach the town through the fields but was intercepted by roughs. My brother was killed, my arm and leg were broken, my skull was fractured, and I was stabbed twice in the side. I fainted from loss of blood, and revived to find a soldier standing over me, who asked: What, are you still alive! Shall I bayonet you?. I begged him to spare my life. The roughs came again but spared me saying: He will die; let him suffer longer.*

The correspondent, who adopts the bitterest tone towards the government, holds that the pogrom undoubtedly was provoked and attributed the responsibility to police lieutenant Shermetieff. He declares that not only the soldiers but their officers participated and that he himself was a witness as late as Saturday to the shooting down of a Jewish girl from the window of a hotel by Lieutenant Miller of the Vladimir Regiment. The governor of the province of Grodno, who happened to be passing at the moment, ordered an investigation.[44]

Even today the catechism of St Philoret of Moscow contains the following explanation:

109. What means the name devil?

It means slander or deceiver.

110. Why are the evil angels called Devils that is, slanderers or deceivers?

Because they are ever laying snares for men, seeking to deceive them, and inspire them with false notions and evil wishes.

> Of this Jesus Christ, speaking to the unbelieving Jews, says:
>
> *"ye are of your father the devil, and the lusts of your father ye will do. He was a murderer from the beginning, and abode not in the truth, because there is no truth in him. When he speaketh a lie he speaketh of his own, for he is a liar and the father of it." John 8.44.*

At the time of the pogroms Tsar Nicholas II, to his credit, was worried that gangs of men were being sent out to put down Jews and a document called the Protocols of the Elders of Zion had to be produced to convince him that the Jews deserved to die. It purported to show that there was a conspiracy by rich Jews to create a global hegemony which would involve the modernisation of Russia and hence the elimination of Tsarist power. It was not an original work of fiction but was based upon the book by Maurice Joly called

---

[44] Mark Twain Reflections on Religion Part 3 Published in 1906

"The Dialogue in Hell between Machiavelli and Montesquieu" was written at the end of the 19th century. The book had a profound effect on anti-Semitism for the next 50 years and is still mentioned in connection with Israel and as a justification for anti-Jewish prejudice. The Protocols are a complete fabrication and their original, The Dialogue in Hell, was written by Joly as a satire in about 1864.

Like the Germans after them, the Russians grew tired of the pogroms as a government way of demonstrating that they were in control so that the Russian government had to send bands of thugs from Moscow to murder Jews to demonstrate they were doing something about the rising price of wheat.[45]

Social Banditry

Closely allied to a common enemy is giving the poor money, even if that money is stolen. This is a form of social behaviour identified by the Marxist historian, Eric Hobsbawm, and which, in its simplest and purest form, is exemplified by the probably mythical figure of Robin Hood who robbed the rich to feed the poor.[46] For bandits of this kind, it is their philanthropy which protects them from arrest and execution in the harsher days of the death penalty. Bandits of this kind prosper in subsistence agricultural economies who are poverty stricken but tied to the land which, in itself, might not even belong to them.

---

[45] Part of the coincidence in the 19th Century was that a global market in wheat came into existence.
[46] Eric Hobsbawm Bandits

One of the earliest examples of social bandits happened to be called Jesus and during an absence of the procurator, Albinus, in Alexandria, in about 62CE, the High Priest, Ananus, took the opportunity to arrest James the brother of the bandit and assembled a Sanhedrin to condemn James to death. This was presumably a rural Sanhedrin because the Great Sanhedrin, who sat in the temple in Jerusalem had power to take evidence in public and condemn a man to death. They were Pharisees and would not have cut corners for a Sadducee. There seems to have been an uproar and those who benefited from Jesus's largesse, met Albinus on the road and got the sentence quashed on the grounds of illegality.[47] It was King Agrippa who actually relieved him of his post.

During his first term in office (1946-1952) Juan Peron, President of Argentina, married a girl who had escaped near destitution called Eva Duarte and who then became Eva Peron. Eva had a flair for politics and coercion. Juan's stated aims were social justices and industrialisation to make Argentina independent of the cold war. These aims he found quite impossible to achieve so that Argentina remained a poor country. Eva created a foundation which coerced money from the rich and gave it to those Eva deemed to be the most needy supplicants. Thousands were given help to alleviate extreme poverty and a hospital was built and staffed for the poor. Nobody asked how much money remained with the Perons themselves. She was referred to as Saint Evita and it would have been considered blasphemy to impute base

---

[47] Josephus Antiquities of the jews Book XX Chapter 9.1.

motives to her efforts. She died of cancer in 1952 while still in her early thirties. Mrs Thatcher, before she became Prime Minister took an interest in Eva's story to see how a woman could rise to such power. One thing she did do which was reminiscent of Evita was to sell to the occupants, Britain's stock of social housing to help pay the fiscal deficit. For many, this sale of property made Mrs Thatcher a benefactor who deserved the loyalty of those she helped into home ownership for her life and beyond.

The present policy of 'levelling up' smacks of social banditry by saying, it seems, 'If you vote for us, we will divert more of taxpayers money in your direction.'

Section 6: Boosting Self Esteem and Social Sadism

William James (1842-1910), the first psychologist at Harvard Medical School, born into a rich and intellectually distinguished family found it impossible to separate a man from his possessions when he talks about self. In American society of more than one hundred years ago, he must be forgiven for thinking about men doing the owning. The Western world was still leaving an agricultural society where a man's superior strength gave him a superior economic position and women are included as possessions.

The factors he does include as inseparable from the male sense of self go as follows: clothes, house, wife, children, ancestors, friends, reputation, works, lands and horses, yacht, bank account and if he loses any of them he feels cast down. This was as good a guide as any in 1900 and defines what James thought of as a gentleman, a man of means. Times change very quickly and by the 1930s, the popular hero was Fred Astaire who was a sharp witted music and dance man and the gentleman was a dim witted fool with inherited wealth. The change can be accounted by a shift in the centre of gravity of money and the cinema goer was a salesman or a factory worker and the hero had to look like him. Change is continuous.

Social Sadism

For those who are made to feel on the fringes of society: closet gays; the poor; Jews; even women and anyone of a different appearance are made to feel, by popular prejudice aimed at them, that they are not in control. Being in control of the environment in which one lives is fundamental to survival. Having a hunting area or land for agriculture has been largely replaced by the arrival of money in about 650 BCE and attributed to King Croesus of Lydia followed by fuel to generate energy which made the industrial revolution possible.

The most primitive, industrial form of fuel was coal followed by oil which have both been used in such quantities that the changes they have caused in the environment are now threatening human survival. For hundreds of years, human beings mistook coinage for wealth until Maynard Keynes in the 1930s, understanding that gold and coinage were valueless, replaced the measure of national wealth with income and the command of credit. He also introduced the idea that, as long as there was slack in the economy measured by unemployment, in his day, then money could be printed for investment to reduce unemployment without causing inflation. Only Roosevelt in the US seems to have listened to him and it gave the US a shot in the arm as it emerged from the bank crash of 1929.

Being in control of the environment a human being lives in is at the essence of human survival and exists shoulder to shoulder with sexuality in it's importance to survival. To take a simple example, if we were desert islanders where some

96

could climb a palm tree to get a coco nut and some could not, then those who could would be in control because they had mastered climbing and hence their environment and those who could not would be subservient to them. A further example might be that if any European were transported to the jungles of Rwanda, he would be unable to find food unaided and would be dead in about five days unless a short black skinned man helped him. The short black skinned man understands and can survive in the Rwandan jungle while the white, educated European does not. It is a matter of life and death. Hence the need for control of the environment we live in and the violence of the language used because losing control puts him closer to death. Sadism and causing pain is about regaining control by the sadist because he is in charge and if lack of control continues long enough without signs of improvement then the victim of lack of control is prepared to kill to regain control. The one doing the abusing is the one who gains or regains control while the abuse goes on.

Staying with Rwanda for a moment, Daniel Jonah Goldhagen, a student of the holocaust was quoted in 'Making Monsters'[48] as saying, with respect to the Rwandan massacre: 'I find it hard to understand, and I want to understand, how people could approach other people who are begging for their lives and screaming with pain, and chop them.' The ones doing the murders were Hutu while the victims were Tutsi who are frequently physically distinguishable but, more importantly, the ex colonial power,

[48]   David Livingstone Smith Making Monsters Page xi

97

Belgium, had issued identity cards stating the holder's ethnic origin: Hutu or Tutsi. This made the Tutsi, as defined by the Belgians, and after inter marriage, quite complicated ethnic rules had to be invented, to make the category clear in a single word which condemned some people, including children, to death or granted life. The same happened in Northern Ireland where the mere label 'Protestant' or 'Catholic' condemned some to death.

Rwanda has two main ethnic groups. The Tutsi are a pastoral people whose wealth is in cattle while the Hutu are agriculturalists whose main cash crop was coffee. In 1990 the coffee market went into free fall and the government had to ask the IMF for a loan which was granted on condition they removed the subsidy on bread in order for the Rwandan government to be able to repay the loan. The first thing a bank asks a humble petitioner is how he is going to repay the loan and Western bankers do not like subsidies. Everything must be subject to the movement of a free market but unable to put bread on the table rendered the Hutu out of control and they were prepared to kill people who did not look like them and to whom a colonial power had ascribed a different label. The Hutu, little more than subsistence farmers, had reached their limit. A cabal of Rwandans, seeing the possibility of gaining power, issued the poor among the Hutu with machetes, radio Mille Collines played patriotic music and the killing began in 1994 and continued for 100 days.

Failing a sufficient income to maintain their way of life many feel out of control of their own lives and without understanding what brought about this sad state of affairs, they resort to a form of sadism by talking to people they trust for example, about how stupid and inadequate black people or women are, even when their own inadequate income has nothing to do with a black person or a woman. This is the extraordinary fact about regaining control; it gives relief to bully someone even weaker than the victim himself. The next stage is to tell black skinned person that they should 'go home' even when they were born in the UK and have never lived anywhere else. Being sneered at in this way is painful but it has to be justified by a generalised myth. In the case of black Americans poverty and lack of opportunity ie prejudice itself, provides the stereotypes which nourish the prejudice into existence in the first place. G S Griffin begins one of his papers on 'racism' as follows:

First, disproportionate black poverty perpetuates white myths of black laziness. Second, black poverty breeds black crime, which reinforces in white minds ideas of the deviant, aggressive, violent black man. Third, black poverty leads to lower academic performance from black children, leading to white myths of lower intelligence in blacks.

All these stereotypes: laziness, violence, and stupidity are imposed on blacks by white prejudice itself denying them opportunity and then used by whites to justify their prejudices. It is the purest example of a vicious circle. Nevertheless, many American and British dark skinned people are people of such ability that they have broken out of the circle and risen to great prominence. The absurdity of this particular prejudice is like saying that if anyone goes for a holiday in the sun, they will return lazy, violent and stupid because the colour of their skin might have changed. Nevertheless, dark skinned players, footballers, particularly those playing for the England team have a lot of invective levelled at them: 'Paki', 'Coon' ,'Black cunt', 'Nigger', 'Monkey chants', 'You fucking Muslim' and on Facebook: 'Muslim cunt'.[49] At the end of Euro 2020 when England lost on penalties to Italy, some England players were booed by their fans as they left the pitch. For some, but by no means all the main purpose of being a fan is to be enhanced by the reflected glory of being a supporter of a winning team. This syndrome exists all over the world and makes selling team gear a goldmine but the team must win. This accounts for the turnover in football managers.

During the pandemic, most were afraid of dying and followed the rules laid down by epidemiologists to avoid spreading the virus. In those circumstances, many feel, quite rationally and reasonably, out of control and resort to abuse. Most resort to throwing imaginary bricks at their television sets but some give vent to their need to abuse via social media and a typical example of sadistic abuse was given in the Guardian newspaper dated 1.1. 2022:

> 'You scaremongering ignorant fucking cunt, you and your retarded team made predictions which could have fucked this country for billions of pounds, fucked Christmas for a second time and cost thousands their jobs only to have your most pessimistic ballshit now found to be just that. How fucks like you can sleep at

---

[49] Reported in The Guardian newspaper 12 April 2019

*night is beyond me and I hope you are fucking held to
account for what you have done if there weren't some
people in the government with a brain.'*

This monologue was directed at Professor John Edmunds,
Epidemiologist at the London School of Hygiene and
Tropical Medicine and member of Sage, via one of his team.
(Not by one of his team). Looking at the content of the
message, the the author of the message is in denial about the
existence of a pandemic in the first place and has invented a
malevolent conspiracy intent on ruining his life including his
Christmas. In this respect, he is no different to senior
politicians who laughed off, initially, the very existence of a
pandemic but were forced by the number of deaths to change
their tune.

Writing or uttering abuse gives the writer a sense of being in
control since sadism is used in any context to provide a sense
of control. The abuser himself feels or is made to feel that
he has failed to reach one of the norms of society laid down
by religion or custom. He regains control by abusing
somebody weaker than himself: women or children are
popular targets of abuse. One of the signs that the abuser is
seeking control can be initially be found in his garden with
stones, raised beds, right angles and paved paths. An
outstanding example of the controlled garden is to be found
in France at Versailles and was completed in 1746 as though
designed by a computer driven spider. By 1790, France was
in chaos. In contrast the English garden, created at about the
same time, by Capability Brown, showed a mansion house
surrounded by moorland, clumps of trees and no fences

101

which echoed English confidence and wealth created by foreign trade. They did not need walls, they were open to everybody.

It would be quite wrong to suppose that shortage of money does not play a major part in abuse. In the year ending May 2022, two and a half million people were having to use food banks but being short of money is not the only source of abuse. A further source of abuse, the author has noticed, comes from those hiding their sexuality. Same sex couples, living normally together, in or out of marriage, are as rational or irrational as anyone else. Those who are bisexual or have married to provide a cover from the prejudices of yesteryear, which are not altogether dead, are the ones who require abuse. It is their frustrated sexuality which fuels their prejudice. One recalls Enoch Powell's homo erotic poetry sitting side by side with his 'rivers of blood' speech which provides an example even though coming from a brilliant mind. It was seized upon by those struggling to maintain their way of life.

Masochism

This human characteristic is displayed by those who turn their sadism back on themselves like self harming which, while the wound is healing, brings order into their lives. The reason for the initial disorder which requires sadism or masochism to restore order can be many and varied but they frequently involve the society they live in directing shame at them. The favoured example of masochism in modern times was Adolf Hitler, the dictator of Germany, and architect of the Holocaust. Hitler's mother was, according to the family's doctor Eduard Bloch, who was incidentally a Jew, a most decent woman and a devout Catholic. Hitler's father was a retired customs official with a uniform denoting his superior rank. A drinker, short of money, who used to beat his feckless son who had silly ideas of becoming an artist instead of going out and earning a livig so that mother had to intervene taking the blows intended for Adolf on her own body. Adolf was her fifth child and hence, her baby. Adolf was devoted to her all his life and kept a portrait of her in every bedroom of his Munich apartment. Sadly, Adolf was a homosexual which is perfectly acceptable and normal in any sane society, but the Catholic church regarded the act, though not the tendency, as intrinsically immoral and evil though they portrayed it, it seems, not a sin. Hitler was actively homosexual during the 14-18 war but denied himself homosexual sex and took up masochistic sex in which he engaged a woman to urinate over him and kick him until he achieved an orgasm. Tragically, his followers were convinced that the public would not understand how innocuous this form of sex can be and so some half dozen young, pretty women were murdered to keep his secret.

Adolf Hitler was a maimed character from the start but the blame for the slaughter of the Second World War must go, if needs be, to the governments, European, American and German, together with the bankers, who humiliated and ruined the German people after 1918. It was far sighted of General Marshall, after the Second World War, to produce a plan which helped to ensure peace in Europe until the present time.

103

This sort of social sadism is designed, it is worth bearing in mind, to bring order into the minds of what would otherwise be normal people and turn them into social sadists. Anyone who is the butt of abuse in normal social circumstances is best advised to cut off communication. This also goes for social media. If this takes the form of personal denigration via social media, then do not read or comment on it. This may well not be easy. In social circumstances then silence is still the best policy this is so even in the case of a stalker who wants to control by appearing in public to be a close friend, and needs to abuse in private. Silence and, where possible, avoidance remain at the top of the list in mild cases. In more severe cases the perpetrator might have to be spoken to by experts and whatever ails him alleviated to the best of one's ability short of renewing contact.

For those who persist on social media, say, the only way might be field work to find out what is really causing them to feel out of control.

There are many examples of social sadism but a typical one is Martin Luther who tried to approach God in a rational way, had common sexuality, found he could not manage without a woman in spite of being a monk, was sympathetic to the Jews, got married and had six children. All this changed when his eldest daughter Magdalena died and he became a Jew hater to alleviate the pain.

Luther was born in 1483 in Saxony, now part of Germany but in those days, part of the Holy Roman Empire during the Renaissance of classical art and Protagoras' saying: Man is the measure of all things. It also involved a break from the narrow legalism of Roman Catholicism. A schism led by Luther called the Reformation.

He was born to, originally peasant, but rose to burgher class parents, Hans and Margarethe Luder which they later changed to Luther. Hans was a leaseholder of copper mines and smelters[50] and decided that Martin should become a lawyer. He went to a school run by lay brothers which taught grammar, rhetoric and logic, 'the trivium', and sounded like the PPE of its day. Luther's mother was a member of the burgher social class and Hans was elevated to mining industrialist and town councillor. Martin Luther seems to have become something of a snob, making clumsy, heavy handed jokes about the peasantry, from which his family sprang, and denouncing the farmers for not bringing food into Wittenberg during plague. As a member of the burgher class social prejudice was part of their way of life.[51] At Erfurt University he broadened his mind and studied Aristotle, gaining his MA in 1505. He suffered from early mood swings, losing the love of Jesus and gravitating away from religion towards the more humanist works of the renaissance. He began a study of law as his father wished but in his reading of the bible he saw a parallel between Hannah in the book of Samuel and his mother having a son dedicated to God. This might be rationalising his decision to follow the rule of St Augustine and become a monk.[52]The life of a monk was marred by periods of severe depression. One episode in the choir he fell down shouting: 'I am not, I am not!'. His

---

50   Martin Brecht referred to in Wikipedia, Martin Luther
51   Michael A. Mullet, martin Luther p.23
52   Mullett pp.33-37

105

depression, it is supposed, was related to fasting and his severe ascetic regime but on another occasion he confessed to 'really serious sins' though what they were is not known but not women.[53] His sins might have been of a homosexual nature. Celibacy is a burden for many people including some priests.

In 1517 he began to have severe doubts about the sale of indulgences, the raising of money to build St Peters in Rome. He preached against it but he was ignored. and he describes himself as the little brother who was despised even though he wrote to the Bishop of Mainz. He finally nailed his ninety five theses to the door of All Saints Church in Wittenberg. They were printed in German in 1518. He also denounced transubstantiation saying it remained real bread and real wine in a sermon of 1519. In 1521 Pope Leo X excommunicated Luther. In 1523 he smuggled 12 nuns out of Nimbschen Cistercian convent and in 1525 he married one of them, Katharina von Bora. She was 26 and he 41.

In 1523 he entered a pragmatic period denying the cult aspects of Catholicism. It was rumoured that he said that Mary was a woman who had many children and Jesus was the son of Joseph but he later denied having made this statement. However, he did so quite light heartedly, even wittily. In the same tract he goes on to cut across one of the tenets of Catholicism of his day ie that the Jews had killed the Christian Saviour and indirectly reaffirm that Jesus was a man born of woman:

---

[53]   Mullett p.44

When we are inclined to boast of our position we should remember that we are but Gentiles, while the Jews are of the lineage of Christ. We are aliens and in-laws; they are blood relatives, cousins, cousins and brothers of our Lord. Therefore, if one is to boast of flesh and blood, the Jews are actually nearer to Christ than we are...[54]

This surge of understanding and benevolence is easy to explain. Luther had met Katharina von Bora and he was in love. They had six children. Their eldest daughter was called Magdalena, a child to whom they were naturally devoted.

By 1525 his benevolence disappeared and his burgher nature reasserted itself. In the Peasants War, a time when the aristocracy broke with Rome to save paying tax, confiscated property and applied taxes to enrich themselves all under the slogan 'German money for a German church', resulted in peasant revolts. The peasants got no sympathy from Luther:

> "*You have to answer people like that until [blood] drips from their noses. The peasants would not listen; they would not let anyone tell them anything, so their ears must now be unbuttoned with musket balls till their heads jump off their shoulders.*"

In 1527 he developed roaring tinnitus in his left ear, vomiting and vertigo symptomatic of Meniere's disease of the left ear which pursued him for the rest of his life until he died in

---

54   Council of Centers on Jewish Christian Relations

1546 of a coronary thrombosis.[55] However, in 1542 his beloved daughter Magdalena, aged 13, died in his arms after a long illness. The account of her death in Wikipedia is very moving and Luther's grief would have been terrible.

A year later, in 1543, he wrote his 65000 word diatribe against the Jews, 'On the Jews and their lies' in which he says their prayer books should be destroyed, synagogues and schools set on fire, rabbis forbidden to preach, homes burned and property and money confiscated. They should be shown no mercy or kindness, afforded no legal protection, and these "poisonous envenomed worms" should be drafted into forced labour or expelled for all time. In the classic manner he was projecting his misery on the Jews, the aliens of his day and making them suffer.

Sporadic outbreaks of the Black Death in Germany acted like the death of Magdalena and drove the anguished Germans to attempt to regain control by genuine hatred and expulsion of Jewish communities. Luther's words have been accused of rationalising the behaviour of the Germans in the Holocaust. The words of Luther might have given some support but it has to be said that the Jews would still have been transported to death camps whether Luther had lived or not and in 1938, the synagogues would still have burned.

Finally social sadism has many names depending on the intended victim. Those in current use are: misogyny, anti Semitism, Islamophobia, homophobia, a general belief in

---

[55]   H. Feldmann in United States Library of Medecine.

stereotypes based on appearance is always misleading, even odious some would say. While they all have different names, they are all entered into by people struggling to maintain their way of life and their sense of control. President Putin might well be struggling to maintain his image as a virile, macho, force to be reckoned with now that he is approaching 70 years. To prove it he started a war against Ukraine.

Section 7: Jew Hatred, The Road to the Holocaust

The Holocaust has been described thousands of times and, for Jews, it is as much a kick in the guts as it was in 1945 when they found out about it and they still do not understand it. However, it is argued here that it was an extreme example of social sadism caused by war and poverty suffered on that occasion by Germany and the crippled mind of Adolf Hitler, the German dictator. Tragically, it was not unique. The Rwandan Hutu hacked their Tutsi neighbours to death with machetes and in 2022 Putin, the Russian dictator sent his army in to Ukraine to murder the inhabitants. The cause for hope is that those sent to do the killing are less and less enthusiastic to kill. Ukraine, in spite of the tragic deaths of young Russians and Ukrainians is a salutary lesson because the whole of Europe and, possibly more, is having to pay for the war which can achieve no more than bolster the ego of an old man. Every nation has old men who behave the same way if left in power or propped in power or both for too long. One has only to think of Robert Mugabe 1987-2017, President of Zimbabwe, who died a natural death, leaving the economy in ruins, at the age of 92. These poor creatures demonstrate the weakness of a dictatorship and the strength of a democracy where much more is subject to debate, though, even this, is not free from error.

At times, following wars, mishandling of the economy, bank collapses, then at such times as those, when the whole population is ruined, social sadism comes to the fore and is directed at those considered a weak minority. In the 1930s, in most Christian countries, it was the Jew. Other countries might have other scapegoats but Christians, once Christianity arrived in Rome, have always homed in on Jews to restore a sense of control to their lives whenever their way of life, or standing in society, was threatened. The Christian saviour, stated in the English gospels to be Jesus of Nazareth, himself began life in Galilee, a Jewish province, some 2,000 years ago. It is said the Jews plotted and murdered him in Jerusalem using the Roman governor as an innocent dupe, reluctant to murder an innocent man.

As a result of this, Jews were murdered in Russia in a series of attacks between 1861 and 1919 and much more severely in Germany between 1938 and 1945. Encouraged by history and the British government, Jews took over Palestine, then a British mandate, after the war with Germany. Britain too had to be removed in order to declare an independent state of Israel with the USA as it's staunchest ally. What follows then is an examination of the veracity of the gospel account of the crucifixion of Jesus and the vehemence and persistence of the hatred which has pursued Jews since then. It must be recognised that had the Christian establishment not directed their social sadism at the Jews, it would have been directed at some other group though not as vehemently, hopefully.

The biblical account of the Jews begins with an account of them being expelled from the Garden of Eden because Eve's fertility totem, a serpent, misled her by urging her to eat the fruit of the tree of knowledge. Jews have been seeking the fruit of the tree of knowledge ever since then and the Hebrew bible is a mixture of myth and history much of which involves a struggle between an invisible all powerful God and the primitive totemic religions which surrounded them. The children of Adam and Havva (Eve in English) Jacob and Esau commemorate their departure from being hunter gatherers to a more pastoral way of life. Moses leads the children of Israel out of slavery in Egypt with the proviso that Freud maintains that Moses himself is a mythical figure[56] and as soon as his back is turned, the Jews revert to a form of fertility faith in the shape of a Golden Calf.[57] The bible has a number of assurances that fertility totems are unnecessary because Jews will be as numerous as the grains of sand on the seashore or the stars in the heavens. What has transpired is that Jews have been the most frequent consumers of the fruit of the tree of knowledge in the world and have won more Nobel prizes than any other ethnic group. As will be recognised, totem worship was widespread throughout the world and round the Mediterranean it was the god of fish and worship in the temple of Dagon which means 'Big Fish'. It will be recalled

---

[56]   Sigmund Freud Moses and Monotheism
[57]   Exodus 32

that Samson the Nazirite destroyed the temple of Dagon once he returned to the true faith.[58] The totems protected the population from illness, provided food and made women fertile so as to increase the population among other things such as bringing victory in battle. To kill the totem was unforgivable because it endangered the whole population.

The bible is an old history written without the rigours of modern scholarship so that archaeology can find no evidence of the Exodus from Egypt for example.[59] The same book as referenced goes on to suggest that nomadic tribes crossed and recrossed the Jordan River year after year until they settled permanently in the hill country to the West of the river and took Jerusalem as their capital. Like all nomads in arid zones, they had to eschew pork because pigs need water. Muslims have adopted the same practice. Contemporary with the arrival of what became the Jews and inhabiting the coastal plain, were the sea people who became the Palestinians and their settlements have abundant pork bone remains. The avoidance of pork was only forced upon them with arrival of the Ottoman Turks. The human population was very small thousands of years ago so that any sexual union that did not result in birth was anathema and women had to be fertile, hence the importance of fertility totems: serpents, golden calves and, more in Italy, bulls.

The North, including Transjordan was less arid and two states developed[60]: one, the city state of Jerusalem, the other,

---

58 Judges 13-16.
59 Israel Finkelstein, The Bible Unearthed p.3.
60 The Bible Unearthed p.155.

the city state of Shechem in which was situated Nazareth inhabited by Nazarenes who became synonymous with Christians.[61] Using Brown Driver and Briggs, Hebrew and English Lexicon p.665 one of the meanings attributed to the root Nun,Tsadek, Resh is, freely translated, taken to mean 'Guardians of the word of God'. Nazarene was therefore, on this meaning, a sect set up possibly in opposition to the rabbinical interpretation of the Pentateuch in Jerusalem. The controversies between Jesus the Nazraya depicted in the gospels are no more than arguments between two philosophies which the Nazarenes generally won and so it might be assumed, they wrote them.

Going back to Aramaic the man we call 'Jesus' in English is someone with a certain moral quality.. His name is spelt Yud Sheen Ayin: Yeshue. Using Brown Driver and Briggs p446 It means Deliverer, someone placed in freedom from Evil by God. On this basis, anyone who strives against evil, wishes to reduce violence to and reducing the suffering of the living is doing the work of God. Jesus is the Jewish everyman and, if this is accepted, did not exist as a physical character but as a carrier of a philosophical message which is as true today as it was thousands of years ago. If so, it is explicable that no outside source can vouchsafe his existence and Eusebius had to insert a passage in Josephus to provide some historical authenticity.[62]

---

61 The Concise Oxford Dictionary of the Christian Faith p252
62 Passage found in Antiqities of the Jews, Book 18 known as Testimonium Flavianum

114

This might explain the encounters between Jesus and the Pharisees. They were arguing about different philosophies, the Nazarenes introducing a humanity focused point of view while the Pharisees remained strict, legalistic interpreters of Mosaic law.

The Aramaic for Matthew is actually Matta, a place in Northern Gallilee, possibly now Syria, near the Mediterranean sea and so Matthew is considered by the Tubingen school to be more significant than the other gospels. Matthew 12 gives an example of the two schools of thought: At that time Yeshue went through the grainfields on the sabbath, his disciples were hungry, and they began to pluck heads of grain and to eat.

The Pharisees protested because it was illegal to do work on the sabbath and in their opinion the disciples were working ie reaping. Yeshue could have made a number of legalistic observations: Was the hunger so severe as to endanger life in which case the transgression would be excused? Did the grain plucked, come from the margins of the field reserved for the poor? Was the grain high enough so as to constitute 'reaping'? All these are factors of consideration in the Talmud. Yeshue the Nazarene confined himself to saying that they were hungry and for this reason only they should be allowed food. This is to say no more than was recognised in the opening of the welfare state in 1945. The Nazarenes were saying the same thing two thousand years earlier when it proved not only popular but had a moral impact which it has never lost. There are a number of other encounters between Jesus and the Pharisees but it would be a major work of scholarship, beyond the capacity of a little book, to describe them all except to say that the Nazarene duty as found in the gospel was to the living and was humanitarian with ritual not being allowed to obstruct a humanitarian act. Nor should any act be obstructed, made illegal or outlawed unless it can be shown to be doing some harm to someone else.

The Nazarene sect were one of the Essenes which were widely distributed in Israel with small colonies in most towns. Their written works were stored at Qumran near the Dead Sea. They became popular among Jews and generations of development can be discerned in the Gospel of Matthew as it was taken up by ethnic group after ethnic group. The Levant had been invaded by Alexander, the Macedonian, on some sort of frolic of his own in the 4th Century BCE.

He left a huge area under the command of the Ptolomies in Egypt and another under the Seleucids which stretched from Egypt to the borders of India so that there were Greek cities dotted around everywhere, one of the largest being Alexandria in Egypt and, smaller but still important, the Decapolis in Israel. The Palestinians continued to hold the coast strip with Juda and Israel held by Jews with the Seleucid hold so weak that a Jewish family called the Maccabees almost pushed them out in 167 BCE.

There was a large diaspora of Jews in both Alexandria and Rome so that Pompey who arrived in Jerusalem in 63 BCE did no more than appoint Jewish puppet kings. Herod, the king, was so obedient at collecting taxes that any Roman assistance he might need came from as far away as Damascus.

Thereafter the land was divided into three: an Ethnarch in Judea; a Tetrarch in Iturea and a Tetrarch in Galilee.

It seems to have been the arrival of the Romans and their requirement of taxes for Rome together with taxes for the king and taxes for the Temple in Jerusalem which broke the back of the poor and rebellions broke out on what seems almost to have been a daily basis and Judea, in particular,appears to have become out of control.

The Jewish Ethnarch, Herod Archeleus was replaced in 6 CE by Coponius. In 9 CE, he was replaced by Marcus Ambibulus, In 12 CE he was replaced by Annius Rufus, In 15 CE he was replaced by Valerius Gratus but in 26 CE he was replaced by Pontius Pilate who lasted until 36 CE. The poverty stricken Jews had good reason to hate the Romans. Gratus faced a major rebellion and had to bring in phalanxes of men from Damascus to subdue the Jews which they did under General Varus who, according to Flavius Josephus, to whom we are indebted for his contemporary accounts of Jewish life, 2,000 Jews were crucified as a warning to the population. The handling of a rebellion with a reign of terror is completely credible of any colonial power.

The Romans built roads in order to move their troops around conquered nations for the same reason the British built railways in India. Again, similar to India, many Jews were happy to bear Roman names, Flavius Josephus is a case in point and rich Jews like Phylo and Agrippa I were educated in Rome and became cosmopolitans. The poor were ground down and started groups of assassins called sicarii. These carried a short dagger and when, in a crowd, they were within range of their target, they struck and killed before disappearing into the crowd. It appears the target was normally a fellow Jew but one who was willing to co-operate with the Romans. These were the Sadducees and Gratus, who needed information from a native because he spoke no Aramaic, recruited Joseph Caiaphus to do his leg work and made him High Priest.

When Pilate arrived in 26 CE he kept Caiaphus on. It is important to understand that the demi-monde which kept Rome in power had nothing to do with the Pharisees who , at that time were chaired by one of the great Jewish teachers and Judges: Rabban Gammaliel who is thought to have died in 52 CE. Rabban Gammaliel chaired the Great Sanhedrin which tried capital offences in the hall of hewn stone at the Eastern end of the Temple entrance. The hall seems to have been open ended so that the general public could follow the proceedings. Caiaphas and Pilate were hated figures because they condemned ordinary Jews to death without trial. It is believed that the Sanhedrin provided a trial in accordance with Jewish law and the accused, if found guilty, was usually stoned to death.

Such capital penalties were rare and, certainly never included crucifixion which was an exclusively Roman penalty. The place of skulls, Golgotha, had posts erected permanently where those condemned to die carried their cross pieces. They were hoisted up the post having been nailed to the cross piece where they are thought to have died of suffocation.

118

Flagellation seems to have taken place at some point in this inhuman procedure. Had the Jews been in charge, he would have had the benefit of a trial and then been stoned if found guilty but just as hard a death. An interesting point arises during the Matthew account of the crucifixion (27.34), the Romans offered Jesus Wine and Gall which he refuses. Such a reference is found in Psalm 69.22, a Psalm of utter despair and in keeping with the Aramaic gospel version of Jesus' last words: 'God God the time has come to let me go' which echoes the words of Elijah when he calls upon God in the wilderness: 1 Kings 19.4, speaking of Elijah, says: "...he himself went a day's journey into the wilderness. He came to a broom bush and sat down under it, and prayed that he might die. Enough! He cried. Now, O Lord, take my life, for I am no better than my fathers."

Elijah appears in Jewish eschatology at the end of the world and this is described in Matthew 27.51.

The reference to gall and wine, with despair seems to be a Jewish insertion to make Jesus the Messiah. However other hands must have made insertions because the resurrection seems to have been a late insertion. It does not appear, for example in the Codex Sinaiticus version of Mark written in the 4th Century.[63]

Pilate, of unknown origin determined to bring Roman law to Jerusalem and moved the army from Caesarea to Jerusalem. He then brought the ensigns with images of Caesar to the

---

[63] Theologians have resolved this by postulating a Gospel Q more or less contemporary with Mark but preceding Matthew. Q has never been found.

gates of the temple and planted them there in contravention of Jewish law which is adamant that no human image should be brought into a place of worship. Jews of Jerusalem lay in his path, bared their necks to be executed and Pilate backed down and took the ensigns away. Pilate undertook and carried out the works for an aqueduct to bring water to Jerusalem though he did use wealth from the Temple which, it seems, Josephus did not approve of. Though the accuracy of what he says need not be doubted, it, again, has to be remembered that Josephus was a Sadducee, the temple acted as a bank and therefore, whose wealth was used to build the aqueduct? Possibly his.

A major insurrection occurred when the Samaritans gathered on Mount Gerizzim, their most holy mountain to listen to a man that Josephus suggests was a mountebank with a remote appreciation of the truth. Pilate stopped the gathering with appreciable loss of life. The Samaritans appealed to the President of Syria, one Vitellius, who dismissed Pilate and, ultimately Joseph Caiaphus at Passover 36 CE. The impression one is left with is that Pilate was somewhat more brutal than even the Romans thought was appropriate. In Josephus there is no sign of modern anti Semitism, merely a small unruly province which had to be controlled from Damascus.

Jesus the Nazarene became a myth of independence and, in the popular mind, a Messiah. This had happened before on several occasions, notably: Judas, the son of Hezekiah in 4 B CE; Simon also in 4 BCE; Athronges, contemporary of the Nazarene, who was poor and a shepherd but physically
120

strong and with four brothers, also tall and strong, declared himself king, won a number of encounters with the Romans and was killed in c27 CE having controlled a small region for, possibly, some thirty years. He was similar to Bar Kochba who came about 100 years later and was also recognised by many as a Messiah. The Nazarene was given by myth every biblical characteristic expected of a Messiah. Many hands have taken part in the writing of the gospels.

Verse 15.4 echoes the Jewish tradition of honouring your father and mother while 12.46-50 leaves mother and brothers standing outside to be ignored looks like a complete contradiction in terms. It can be explained by saying that 12.46-50 was added several hundreds of years later when the then new religion was being sold to the Romans and Jesus was deserting his family, behaving like Aeneas, deserting Dido to devote himself to his new duty in Rome.

The Jews, as was their custom, adopted those who were freeing their country from the oppression of Roman taxation as heroes so that the terrorist Simon bar Giora who took Jerusalem in order to evict the Romans in the year 70 became a hero named Jesus and Simon Peter. Jesus apostles were 'sent out', they were sent out to defend the walls of Jerusalem and ten of them appear in the writings of Flavius Josephus always remembering that Josephus was a Sadducee who had money and thought opposition to Rome was futile. Simon was the son of a plasterer who used crushed stone and Simon's name was transmuted to Simon son of stone or Simon Peter in Greek. At the last supper, which was a pagan version of a Jewish ceremony Jesus knows one of his apostles will betray him according to the gospels. This apostle turns out to be Judas Iscariot according to the gospels, a treacherous Jew or Judas ben Judas according to Josephus who thoroughly approves of him. Judas ben Judas, one of the Sicarii, is in charge of one of the towers on the wall and he realises that the defence of Jerusalem is a hopeless task. He and his most reliable followers call to the Romans below to surrender but they cannot believe their ears and do nothing.

When Simon bar Giora hears about this perfidy he tips Judas and his followers from their towers to the ground below. According to Acts of the apostles , their innards burst open and the area becomes known as' the field of blood'. Simon bar Giora was captured and transported to Rome where he was executed by throwing him off the Tarpeian Rock, a cliff face in Rome. This event was commemorated in legend by saying that Simon Peter was crucified upside down. This could have been Jewish or Greek/Christian Legend.[64] The story of Jesus seems to move away from the doctrine of the Nazarenes which had a humanity we can only admire today and try to emulate to simply, in part, replacing the totemic pagan religion of old. Whilst, for many Jesus, replaced the totems of their early, primitive faith and The Gospel of John, written in the 2nd Century introduced the idea that Jesus was a god[65] In some Italian churches a statue of a porcelain white man, pouring blood from wounds, stands against the wall. James Carroll in his book Constantine's Sword (2001) describes a German Passion Play where Jesus, his head

---

[64] The muddle in the history of this period is discussed in more detail in Roger Nelson, Notes on Abuse Section 7.
[65] Tertullian 155-200 AC but there are several others.

crowned in matted blood, wilts under the whipping the 'Jews' give him wearing conical hats and behaving like emissaries of the Devil. After the Holocaust the performance was modified to be less filled with Jew hatred. Bad and inaccurate it may have been, it cannot, on it's own account for the degree of savagery the Germans and others showed the Jews and others during the Second World War. It has to be remembered that following the misery of war or famine, many people have their lives thrown out of control and they regain control by a sadistic onslaught on a group they have been taught to regard as being weaker than them selves and worthy of punishment. The story of the crucifixion, told as drama, set the Jews up for a sadistic onslaught on the basis that, having murdered the Christian Saviour, they deserved what they got. It is on this basis that, at Easter, the crucifixion of Jesus is celebrated to this day.

The preliminary to the holocaust begins, like many acts of evil, in war. The cost of modern warfare is such that if the war is not over quickly, the cost has to be transferred to the general public and, whether the winner or loser, it seems to make little difference. Both have to suffer and pay. In 1870, A Hohenzollern was to become head of state in Spain. Possibly in pursuit of a balance of power in Europe, France was provoked by Von Bismark into going to war against Prussia, a war which France lost in six weeks.

The French ceded Alsace Lorraine and a large indemnity. War was seen as providing both funds and land in which the people spoke German. In fact the inflow of funds overheated the Prussian economy and the resulting period of austerity

123

to bring inflation under control caused a wave of Anti Semitism and increased poverty for the poor. Of no real benefit to anyone. Nevertheless, the Franco Prussian war became a model: It was short; the victor gained territory, in this case Alsace Loraine, Bavaria, Wurtemburg and Baden. The loser paid compensation and war was short and decisive. At the end of the conflict 1870-71 the French paid Prussia 5 billion francs and the stock exchange went wild. Property prices increased 600 fold and middle class Germans were prepared to take bigger and bigger risks until the Viennese banks failed and then their securities became valueless and the middle classes became insolvent. This struck at the control they thought they had of their environment and they rounded on the Jews using sadism to regain control. A jew called Henry Bethel Strousberg had made himself very rich and he became the personification of all Jews.

War is a nation's extension of diplomacy by other means. It always sounds fine but what was not then understood until the 20th Century was that money does not exist, only credit and trade define a nation's power. Trade in manufactured goods was replacing agriculture in importance but it was a hard lesson to learn for peoples brought up on the battle fields of Europe and the transition from sovereignty to trade is still continuing in the 2020s nearly 150 years later. The great powers were acknowledged to be Britain, France, Russia, Austria-Hugary and Germany based on the size of their armies and their trade. America, at that time, stayed out of Europe and confined their overseas influence to the Council of Ten[66] as the rich nations drifted into another war, known as the Great War.

The war was set by the assassination of the Crown Prince Franz Ferdinand in Sarajevo by a man called Gavrilo Princip who came across the Crown Prince and his wife by accident after their car took a wrong turning. Princip fatally wounded them. Europe was ready for war with 2 million Frenchmen under arms and even the British and the Belgians with 100,000 men each. The Germans might have had 1.7 million and so the Germans were outnumbered and foolish to go to war as governments always are. Ponsonby and the Quakers wanted the UK to stay out of it but some individuals had given their word and Henry Wilson prepared and put in the field an expeditionary force under Sir John French. The Germans had modified the Schliefen plan of attack under the direction of von Moltke and they attacked through Belgium in August 1914. The French were in charge of the war first with Joffre, then with Nivelle and finally with Petain. The war bogged down, literally, on the Marne river plain with the British expeditionary force holding the line in front of Paris with the third entente partner, Russia, who were ordered by the French to take Konigsberg (Now Kaliningrad) in East Prussia.

This, they were quite unable to do and the Germans drove them back to the Brest Litovsk line (Now in Belarus) where the Russians/Bolsheviks capitulated in March 1918. The

66   David Stevenson 1914-1918 The History of the First World War pp.33, 746 Penguin books.

Germans won the battle of Tannenberg near the village of that name where the Poles and the Lithuanians had defeated the Teutonic Knights in 1410 and rose to mythic proportions in the Kaiser's mind as the revenge of Germany for the defeat of the Teutonic Knights who were, by what accounts there are, to be no more than a military order taking protection money from pilgrims travelling to the Holy Land. The Russians were defeated at Tannenberg because the French ordered the Russians to persist with an attack to relieve pressure on them. They took 91,000 men in dead and wounded and General Samsonov took his own life. The importance of this pointless battle lay in that it propelled Generals Hindenburg and Ludendorf to the fore, Hindenburg failed to understand the altered nature of the war and kept searching for an army big enough to breach the entente defences and take France. Only the British maintained the blockade of the North Sea, mining the straits of Dover thereby driving shipping to the Kentish coast where it could be stopped and searched. At the same time British warships manned by the Royal Navy Voluntary Reserve (RNVR) maintained a blockade, 365 days a year, of the waters off the Orkneys and the coast of Norway until the Germans sued for peace when substantial numbers of Germans in the field capitulated.

Hindenburg had contributed to the defeat of the German army by taking every man off the land and putting him in uniform in an increasingly desperate attempt to bring about a break through but it was in vain. British women were prepared to work on the land but there are no reports that German women were prepared to do the same so that agricultural production, if anything, fell. With imports of food cut off by the blockade, families were writing to their men at the front begging them to bring the war to an end by any means possible regardless of whether Germany won or lost.

Whatever the reason, it is certain that German morale collapsed in 1918. What is clear is that the collapse of the Russian army in 1917 gave rise to a victory frenzy among the troops[67] but this was short lived. It was expected by the men in the trenches that British and French resistance would stop and they would capitulate and, at the very least, ask for an armistice. This did not happen and by May 1918 sentiment was turning against Ludendorff, the field commander by Social Democrat Heinrich Aufderstrasse who gave a speech addressed to Ludendorff which amounted to: In God's name Go![68]

This soon became known as the stab in the back and defeat had been brought about by the Jews though there was no evidence of this. Quite the contrary: a survey by the Prussian government showed that Jews were present in the army in the same proportion as they were present in the population[69]. An example of attributing tragedy and misfortune to people who do not look like us or speak like us. The loss of the war in 1918 came as a complete impossibility by all the combatants and General Ludendorf had laughed in disdain when he heard America had entered the war.[70] But the

---

67   German Soldiers in the Great War p.217
68   Ditto p.216
69   The Jew Count
70   Alexandra Richie Faust 's Metropolis p.450

Germans did bring about a coup by financing revolution in Russia which has been estimated at 50 million Deutschmarks.[71] The German command still had no idea they had lost the war and as late as March 1918 had visions of a vast Eastern empire from the Baltic to the Ukraine.[72] The Kaiser handed over to Max von Baden who, on 4/5 October, sent a note asking for an armistice which was granted. Unnecessarily, the blockade was continued into 1919 causing more German hardship.

At the Versaillles conference, 1919-1920, The Germans thought they would negotiate around some points which Woodrow Wilson had set out as the basis for peace. In the event they were not allowed to open their mouths and the conference was a diktat.

Curiously, one of the factors which jeopardised the sense of security and being in control in the German mind was not simply that they had lost the war but that they then proceeded to lose the peace. In the 19th Century, Bismarck (1815-1898) the unifier of Germany, had instituted a welfare state as a sop to the working class but it became a factor which made Germany, by the end of the 19th Century, one of the industrial power houses of the world. It included pensions, accident insurance and unemployment benefits.[73] Bismarck was dismissed by Kaiser Wilhelm II, a somewhat childish person who simply did not understand either economics or

---

[71]   Richie, p.456
[72]   Richie, p.456
[73]   Harry Harmer Friedrich Ebert: Germany Makers of the Modern World.
p128

the world he lived in, and went to war in 1914 without understanding the ruinous cost of modern warfare.

Maynard Keynes in his book The Economic Consequences of the Peace describes the main characters at the Versailles Peace Conference as: Clemenceau the French leader, an old fashioned nationalist who was only interested in what benefited France, regardless of the rest of the world; Lloyd-George who was sophisticated and wordly; Woodrow Wilson, who,while looking down on the Europeans, was intent on behaving with integrity. Clemenceau was only interested in obtaining reparations from Germany for France. Keynes spends most of his book showing that the reparations demanded were grossly inflated and that Germany could not afford to pay them in any event. Germany had, at the end of the war 2.7 million injured soldiers who, under the terms of the welfare state, had to be cared for. Ebert started printing money probably in the knowledge that the country was bankrupt as were France and Italy. Germany spent half her gold reserves by the end of 1919 and in1922 announced that she could not pay reparations so that, to avoid bankruptcy, in 1923 France occupied the Ruhr and took control of the Key industries. The reparations were seen as vital to France but the continued printing of money to keep the domestic economy and the 'welfare' enjoyed by Germans afloat, produced inflation. What Europe needed was free trade stimuli but instead went on to the Gold Standard, including Britain, which, at a stroke, reduced inflation to 2% and made some currencies very expensive and exports unaffordable. Stripping out exports from a nations economy caused massive unemployment which rippled around the world and slowed trade almost to a standstill.

With the lives of millions of Germans taken out of control by losing the war, having the terms of the so called peace treaty dictated to them, the French occupation of the Ruhr, massive inflation, the disappearance of their pensions, left many Germans in a state where the only route back to control was to kill and the Gospels pointed squarely at the Jews.

John Dominic Crossnan in his book "Who Killed Jesus: Exposing the Roots of Anti-Semitism", in the Gospel Story of the Death of Jesus.

The verse in Matthew which Crossnan homes in on is 27:24-25 When Pilate saw that he could do nothing but rather that a riot was beginning, he took water and washed his hands before the crowd, saying, *'I am innocent of this man's blood; see to it yourselves.'* Then the people as a whole answered, *'His blood be on us and on our children'*.

Taken at face value, this damns the Jews for all time for the death of the Christian Saviour but the first thing that strikes the observer is that the mere washing of hands, essential before eating, would never be enough to wash away a sin as grave as the death of an innocent man. Jeremiah 2.22 makes this clear:

"For though thy wash thee with nitre, and take thee much soap, yet thine iniquity is marked before me," saith the Lord God.

130

"The Essenes, from whom according to many scholars, Jesus the Nazarene sprang, believed in the power of water to purify from sin."[74]

The book of Jeremiah is not chosen by accident by people of that period, since the prophet loathed King Zedekiah, a Babylonian appointee there is a parallel with Pontius Pilate who was a Roman appointee and Joseph Caiaphas, a Sadducee, who was his henchman and who took innocent men into custody. If Pilate found himself unable to carry out the death sentence which, under Jewish law he had no power to do, then Jesus would have had to be handed over to the Sanhedrin or released. The Sanhedrin, at that time, was chaired by Rabban Gamaliel a much admired and upright Pharisee who, even though he was trying a Nazarene, might well have let him go. If the Nazarene was to die then it was the Roman, Pilate, who had to condemn him to death but it was within his power to release him and so he chose to proceed with the crucifixion after scourging him which was the normal, savage Roman procedure. The normal Jewish procedure would have been to stone him to death but this never arose because it was not certain the Sanhedrin would have considered any sort of capital offence appropriate since he had committed no offence recognised by Jewish law. Indeed, he had committed no offence, so far as appears in the gospels, against Rome which took alarm at any kind of insurrection. In this respect, Pilate has form.

The Samaritans arranged via an unknown man resident in the village of Tirathaba to go up Mount Gerizzim to view some

---

[74] Geza Vermes The Dead Sea Scrolls p147.

ancient vessels which, he alleged, Moses had buried there. Pilate prevented the crowd from going up with a band of horsemen and foot soldiers. They killed some and put others to flight. When he captured some of them he ordered them to be put to death . The Samaritan senate appealed to Vitellius, President of Syria, accusing Pilate of murder because it was a peaceful gathering and there was no question of an insurrection against Rome. Vitellius sent his friend Marcellus to replace Pilate and Pilate was returned to Rome to face an enquiry for murder.[75] It has to be said, on this account, that Vitellius had been Consul in (possibly) Samaria so that he knew Pilate was a doubtful character. (Again, in order to sell the new religion to Rome, the historical Pilate has to be scrubbed up and turned into a rather weak willed but, basically, decent chap.)

There remains the question of who were those who called for the death of Jesus? The common people loathed the Romans and to some extent, the High Priest, to whom they paid taxes though Pilate on one occasion built an aqueduct using stolen money, from the point of view of some, which did not make him popular. The great bulk of Jews would not have called for the death of the Nazarene who, judging by his exchanges with the Pharisees, made him their hero. Nor would the Pharisees, under the guidance of Gamaliel, have called for the death of an innocent man. A further factor which would have affected the sentiment of common people to the crucifixion of Jesus is the description of the miraculous healing power which, it is claimed, Jesus has.[76] This would have made the

---

75   Flavius Josephus, The Antiquities of the Jews Chapter 4.
76   See, for example, Matthew 8 and 9

new religion very popular with non Jews and Jesus's death all the more terrible.

When Christianity reached Rome various cults were taken over and about 400 AC resurrection was added before the end of the world and eunuchs required in some resurrection cults were replaced in Christianity by celibate priests, though, it has to be said that the Nazarene himself, as an Essene, might have been celibate.

The only group who might have called for the death of Jesus are what we would call the 'well-to-do'. There is a story, again from Josephus, which illustrates this possibility.

In the days of Albinus, Procurator 62-64 CE, a disturbed man called Jesus the son of Ananus, a plebeian and a husbandman, suddenly started to cry aloud: 'A voice from the East, a voice from the West, a voice from the four winds, a voice against Jerusalem and the holy house, a voice against the bridegrooms and the brides, and a voice against the whole people.'

His constant warning got on the nerves of decent middle class people who referred their problem to Albinus who prepared to chastise him. He went on repeating this dirge even when whipped until his bones were laid bare, nor did he ever explain himself or ask for mercy until Albinus judged him to be a harmless madman and released him. The major rebellion began in 70 CE and Jesus kept repeating his dirge while walking round the walls of Jerusalem until, by chance, a stone from a Roman catapult hit him on the head and killed him.

In spite of the lateness of the events described by Josephus, after the Nazarene is thought to have died, it is not impossible that the sad existence of this Jesus flavoured the Gospel stories.

There is no outside reference to the physical existence of the Jesus of the Gospels to such an extent that Eusebius, the librarian at Tiberius is said to have forged an insertion in to the 'Antiqities of the Jews' in order to provide some historical basis for him. The jury is still out and the Nazarene might still be a construct, a Jewish Everyman, whose crucifixion provided the basis for Christianity and therefore difficult to relinquish. What is certain is that the humanity with which the Nazarene dealt with the everyday problems of his time makes him one of the great thinkers human beings have ever produced. The Tubingen School argues convincingly that Christianity is a synthesis between Jewish Christianity and Gentile Christianity. Tragically, whatever the truth, when the horrors of war and subsequent mismanagement of the European economy together with the French need for reparations, humiliated and starved the Germans, Christianity, as understood by clergymen who were also suffering the same misery, pointed the finger at the Jews and the anti Jewish sadism needed, in their minds, to restore control. Sadism directed at other people, people other than the Jews, who were also stereotyped as weak and undesirable such as Slavs and Roma. These too were made slave labourers or consigned to the death camps.

The massive unemployment in Germany which led to the need of Germans to regain control, was presided over by Chancellor Ebert. Germany, having been reduced to poverty

134

by the occupying French was then assailed by a communist organisation called the Spartacists. Ebert's control of the country seems to have been limited and so he recruited a vigilante force of veterans, largely unpaid by the state but what pay they got came from an extreme right wing group who became the National Socialists or Nazi Party. The veterans were finally called the Freikorps, a private army, owing allegiance to the Nazi Party and their task was to restore order on the streets by killing communists and Jews, none of whom finally got any protection from the state.

Nor did they get much sympathy from the German people because their own poverty, loss of pensions and work left sadism as their only means of restoring control. After some 600 years of anti Semitism, was institutionalised and the Jews were the prime target. The Communists came a close second, identified as they were by the German government as another enemy within. Indeed the two merged in the lower class German mind aided by the fact that one or two of the leading Spartacists and Bolsheviks were Jews.

The ending of the French occupation of the Ruhr and the adoption of the Dawes Plan, both in 1925, effectively liberated German production of iron and steel together with freedom from the threat of reparations allowed German industry to grow. Hjalmar Schacht (1877-1970) became economics minister. He cured hyperinflation by the invention of a new unencumbered currency called the Rentenmark based on the mortgage value of all German property and he founded IG Farben. He is normally credited with the German economic miracle. While the hard work of restoring Germany's economy was going on, right wing parties were vying for control offering no more than social sadism as an inducement to get the public to vote for them. One of the most convincing speakers was a flawed individual called Adolf Hitler (1989-1945) who has been studied with incredulity in over one thousand books.

Hitler was an Austrian the son of a pompous bully of a customs official who married and slept with the young maid servant whoever she was. He did this three times as two wives died and his third wife, Klara, previously his maid servant, gave birth to Adolf. Adolf seems to have been her fifth child and was, like the rest of mankind, bisexual but tended more to the homosexual end of the spectrum. The Judeo Christian churches looked down on homosexuality, even describing it as a sin and in some regimes, Britain, for example it was a criminal offence. Hitler, like many others, concealed his true sexuality. As a young man, he had a flair for art and his drawings of buildings are good and detailed but no more than that. The Viennese art teachers and professors suggested a profession as an architect but there was no money for such a profession to be pursued and he scratched a living in Vienna drawing postcards for sale to tourists. He drifted and , at the age of 25 found himself in Germany when the First World War broke out and he was drafted into the List regiment on the Ypres salient. Possibly for the first time, he enjoyed his true sexuality with other soldiers. His mother was an observant Catholic and though she died in 1907 of cancer he must have felt he had let her down particularly when, looking back, she was the only woman who ever loved him. His lack of control over the life he lived caused him to gain control through sadism sometimes directed inwardly towards himself as will be seen. His social sadism accentuated his lack of empathy for his fellow human beings which has been noticed in his artwork, but he lacked empathy particularly in the case of Jews. As has been considered earlier Jew and Communist hatred made him popular and whilst not the sharpest tool in the box, that slot must go to Goering, he became considered indispensable to the Nazi Party.

Towards the end of the war, the constant artillery bombardment, the fear and the noise caused him to develop hysterical blindness, believing, sincerely, he had been blinded by mustard gas though there was no gas attack at the time in question. The man who treated him was a psychiatrist called Edmund Forster who was told to take his own life when Hitler rose to power. This he did to save his family, there had to be no evidence that the idol of Germany and pillar of the party, might be seen to have been a coward during the war. He had to be an unblemished veteran of that terrible war. Upon the war being lost, Adolf recovered his sight though this was normal in the case of mustard gas on many occasions.

Hitler reverted to drifting but, by chance, he became a celebrity. Like any modern celebrity, he was just like everyone else only more so. He had fought in the war; he held the Iron Cross First Class, he was poor. What did distinguish him were his flashing blue eyes and his riveting manner of delivering a speech of the 'I am going to make Germany great again'

137

variety and he was going to do it by grinding Germany's enemies into the dirt. This coincided with the sentiments of many of the German people who were left feeling out of control by their poverty were ready to take control by force. Ironically this was just about the time when the Dawes Plan and Schacht's economic miracle was beginning to bear fruit. Ian Kershaw, one of Hitler's biographers says of him, even before he became Chancellor:

> *The themes of his speeches varied little: the contrast of Germay's strength in a glorious past with its current weakness and national humiliation-a sick state in the hands of traitors and cowards who had betrayed the Fatherland to its powerful enemies; the reasons for the collapse in a lost war unleashed by these enemies, and behind them the Jews; betrayal and revolution brought about by criminals and Jews; English and French intentions of destroying Germany, as shown in the Treaty of Versailles- the "Peace of Shame", the instrument of Germany's slavery...*[77]

Emotional speeches like this, devoid of credible facts had the desired effect and the Nazi party seized power, led by Hitler under the direction of Goering, on 30 January 1933 followed by elections on the 5 March 1933. In spite of ignoring any democratic process and using violence in January, the Reichstag fire trial and smashing in the windows of Jewish shops, the Nazis won 43.9% of the popular vote and became the largest single party with 288 seats against the SPD, KPD and at least three other parties, all of whom gained seats,

---

[77] Ian Kershaw Hitler 1889-1936: Hubris. Quoted in Friedrich Ebert: Germany

there can be no doubt that Hitler was the popular choice and his overt anti Semitism, whether genuine or not, made him the leader of free and democratic choice so that, what followed, can be laid at the door of the German people of that time. Hitler's modus operandi was to sign peace treaties with several European nations including Czechoslovakia, Poland and Russia and then invade and conquer. Famously, when invading Russia, he found the country was too immense for a lightning strike and Russia slowly gathered strength and defeated the German army at Stalingrad in February 1943 but Hitler could not surrender. With the sole exception of the United Kingdom, every other European country, even France, had capitulated following the first lightening strike of the Panzer divisions.

The out of control damage to Hitler's personality was extensive. Out of respect for his mother's faith in Catholicism, he stopped having sex with men and turned his sexual needs in on himself. Hoffman, his photographer held parties at which pretty women made themselves available for important men. When Hitler got them back to his Munich apartment where there was a portrait of his mother Klara in every bedroom, he wanted them to urinate over him while he masturbated. Understandably many of them refused and were assassinated by Hitler's closest henchmen in order to keep his secret. The success of the Nazi party depended on this hopelessly inadequate man and women who found his requirements too distasteful. Gelli Raubel, his niece, said she had to squat over his face and then urinate or more. He seems to have been grateful to her and bought her lavish presents but when she intended to leave him for a more normal life with another man she was found dead with a pistol she did

139

not own beside her. Hitler himself was very upset. It is not known whether he was even consulted. The survival of the party had to come first.[78]

Hitler's rise to power was based largely on legitimising sadism against the Jews and, instead of being a criminal offence, it was almost encouraged, with the German police looking on as Jews were made to scrub the pavement, had their beards tweaked and other indignities. When the Germans invaded Poland, they started murdering civilians, the majority of them Jews. With the vagaries of war and fear of death this was intended to give some illusion of being in control but even so, it seems a substantial number of Germans were reluctant to machine gun villagers sitting on the edge of excavations they had dug themselves. The Wehrmacht were relieved of this particular form of murder and 'Police Battalions' of middle aged men were recruited in Germany to carry on.[79] After Stalingrad, the total defeat of the German army seemed inevitable, Hitler went into hiding and Himmler took over. After February 1943, Germany had lost the war but in order to conceal the fact, Himmler opened more death camps to show the people they were patriotic and actively engaged in ethnic cleansing while Goebbels made films showing how disgusting the Jews were (Jew Süs) and the extent to which Germany was winning the war. For Germans actually doing and close to the fighting, these messages were stale but the films were so good that many Germans were surprised to find they had lost.

---

[78] Robert G I Waite The Psychopathic God Adolf Hitler Chapter 3.
[79] Daniel Joseph Goldhagen, Hitler's Willing Executioners, Chapter 8.

Albert Speer, the architect, conducted armaments production in order to find a super weapon which would kill in such numbers that it would win the war. This they very nearly did in the shape of rockets which were fired at London. The slaughter of Germans and Russians continued on the Eastern Front; civilians in death camps and, after June 1944, the Western Front where American and British troops fought a more mechanised war towards Berlin. After Stalingrad, it was clear to many German people that the war was going very badly for them and they lost interest in Nazi propaganda, death camps, evil Jews and the rest of the showmanship.

What was clear was that if they were sent to the Eastern front, they were going to die and only Himmler and the Gestapo kept a semblance of resistance. The war ended with Hitler's suicide in 1945 and the American General Marshall, instead of seeking reparations gave aid on a massive scale to Western Europe including Germany. Nobody, it seems, wins a modern war. The number of dead in World War II ran into tens of millions, a number too horrible to go on counting.

What can be postulated very clearly is that the period of extreme hardship starting with the loss of the First World War, the French invasion of the Ruhr followed by Ebert's attempt to carry on as 'normal' with Hindenburg's rudimentary welfare state rendered the country bankrupt. Germans felt totally out of control so that the less intelligent saw the only way of gaining control was through sadism because when when you are inflicting pain, you are in control.

Indeed Himmler was a real sadistic Psychopath and was sent snuff movies from the death camps by a couple, he described himself as a doctor, of inmates breathing their last breath. Himmler sent them colour film for this purpose. Himmler had them assassinated as the war ended. He had hopes of becoming the leader of a post war Germany, oblivious of the enormity of his crimes, but a British soldier recognised him and he bit on his cyanide tablet. Goering did the same after being found guilty of war crimes at the Nuremburg trials. He protested his innocence by saying: 'We did not invent anti-Semitism!' True, but you helped lead the losing side. He was the minister in charge of the Luftwaffe and made every mistake it was possible to make including the horror of the Blitz and a total failure to provide an air lift to supply General Paulus at Stalingrad. Many not too clever Alpha males whose way of life is threatened for whatever reason, sometimes nothing more than advancing years, abandon their wives and marry a younger woman, or, occasionally, a man.

A recent tragic example has been given by President Putin, dictator of Russia, who, on reaching the end of his seventieth year, invaded Ukraine to show he is still in control. Old age is not at all unusual and most people cope with it, when the old person is an absolute monarch or a dictator, they can be a danger as they lose control and use violence to regain control. One of the great strengths of democracy is that it enshrines debate and freedom of speech. In 2019 the Prime Minister, Mr Johnson asked the Queen to prorogue parliament. On appeal to the Scottish court, Inner House of the Court of Session, it was decided that the prorogation was an attempt to stifle the scrutiny of parliament and it was quashed. It will be recalled that Mr Johnson was elected on a platform which consisted of little more than the agreement with the social sadism of many of the British people, in order to achieve Brexit. The difficulty with resorting to the law, it is, like the Ritz Hotel, open to everybody, but only the very rich can afford it. A more available system is required for ordinary people which used to be available through an MP or an ombudsman and possibly it still is in some cases.

It is suggested here that once the underlying lack of control is dealt with, the sadism will disappear and that particular human being will behave in a more rational manner. One way to test this would be to ask for volunteers who have posted abusive comment on social media to submit themselves to a conversation with a skilled observer under a promise of anonymity. The result could then be published without names. Once the general public grasped the power of social sadism in their own minds, it might begin to disappear and we would have a less violent society. The contemplative religions like the Quakers put a brake on violent language by meeting and sitting in silence to pray. This is said to lower the activity of those parts of the brain where violence is seated and lead to the use of moderate language. One can only hope that that has proved to be the case here.